The
CHINTZ
Collectors Handbook

Francis Joseph
ISBN 1-870703-03-0

Acknowledgments

Many people assisted in compiling this book and thanks go to the following: Susan Scott for much additional information; to both Marcia Sutton from Australia and Christine Cope for supplying many of the photographs; to James Kent and Royal Winton for pictures of reissued chintz and finally to Beverley, Beth and others who have provided the prices and the price guide for the book. Most particularly, thanks to Muriel Miller whose original research into Royal Winton was indispensable and forms the basis of this book.

© Francis Joseph Publications 1999
First edition

Published in the UK by
Francis Joseph Publications
5 Southbrook Mews, London SE12 8LG

Typeset by E J Folkard Print Services
199 Station Road, Crayford, Kent DA1 3QF

Printed in Great Britain by Greenwich Press Ltd
Standard House, Eastmoor Street, London SE7 8LX

ISBN 1-870703-03-0

Contents

Royal Winton – The Rolls Royce of Chintz

Colour Gallery of English Manufacturers

Pattern and Price Guide

The Grimwade (Royal Winton) Company

The firm of Grimwade Brothers was founded in 1885 at the Winton Pottery, Stoke-on-Trent, by Leonard Lumsden Grimwade and his elder brother, Sidney Richard. The factory originally consisted of a shed sited between two rows of cottages but business was brisk and it was not long before the firm expanded.

In 1887, the Winton Hotel was built featuring new showrooms. It was sited close by Stoke Station and was convenient for visiting buyers who travelled by rail. The company's turnover doubled each year and by 1890, a flourishing export department was established with the company taking a London showroom at Ely Place, Holborn.

To cope with this development of trade, a new Winton Pottery was built in 1892. This was a large building set on the main road and had the added advantage of being only a three minute walk from Stoke Station. The building had a frontage of 180 feet and a four storey elevation. It contained some of the most up to date equipment to be found in the potteries at that time and, over subsequent years, the area at the rear was built up with a network of kilns, ovens and workshops. The total area covered was almost two acres.

The showrooms were sited in London at 3-5 Charterhouse Street, Holborn Circus and by 1889, had moved to Ely Place, Holborn.

In March 1900, the Stoke Pottery, owned by James Plant, was acquired with Plant being given a place on the Grimwades Board as a director. The Stoke factory was adjacent to the Trent and Mersey Canal and, apart from the large range of ovens and kilns, also included complete equipment for milling the raw materials, including flint and Cornish stone. The three potteries (Grimwade Bros, Winton Pottery and Stoke Pottery) were then amalgamated under the title of Grimwades Limited with Leonard Grimwade as chairman.

In that same year, the Grimwade brothers left Ely Place and purchased the lease on 13 St Andrew Street, a corner site at the conjunction of St Andrew Street and Shoe Lane in Holborn Circus, London. Winton House, as it was known, then became their main showroom.

Back in Stoke, Leonard Grimwade experimented with new methods of kiln-firing and developed enamel firing of high quality with the use of Climax Rotary Kilns.

New showrooms were erected at the Winton Pottery in Hanley in 1906. To achieve these, three cottages in Newland Street were pulled down and a three-storey building was erected. It was opened by the Mayor of Hanley on the 25th of October.

Expansion continued at a great pace.

Yours faithfully
Leonard L Grimwade

Chairman of the Board.

Brownfield's Works, carried on by The Upper Hanley Pottery in Woodall Street, Cobridge, were acquired in 1906, the factory being 'particularly adapted for trade with Canada, the United States of America and other important foreign markets'. Later in the same year, Atlas China (formerly David Chapman & Sons) in Wolfe Street was purchased, enabling the company 'to cater for their many customers who required high-class China Tea Sets at moderate prices especially suited to a cultured taste'. The Heron Cross Pottery at Fenton, owned by Messrs Hines Bros, was an extensive earthenware pottery with extra large ovens and several enamel kilns and this was bought the following year, adding considerably to the company's facilities. (It was later sold to Cartwright & Edwards in 1916.) Grimwades also acquired the Rubian Art Pottery Ltd in 1913.

Export trade was also on the up with the company having agents in Australia, New Zealand, Canada, India, South Africa, South America, United States of America, Sweden, Norway and Germany. By 1920, Egypt had been added to the list.

In 1908, Leonard Grimwade bought shares in the Chromo Transfer and Potters' Supply Co Ltd. This company, which was situated at one end of the Winton Pottery factory, provided 'chromo and lithographic transfers, ceramic colours, potters' materials, glazes and the like'. They were also responsible for the development of 'Duplex' paper, a thin printing tissue which made the lithograph process easier.

Leonard Grimwade also purchased the patent rights of the Grimwade Rotary Display stands around 1913. These were 'Made of finest steel, double-plated metal parts, stained wood shelves' and could accommodate '12 half tea sets, 12 cover dishes and plates, or 12 ewers and basins'. The stands were used for shop display and economised on space. Also, 'ware can be displayed so effectively that assistants are able to increase sales and serve customers far more expeditiously.'

Patent 'Ideal' Display Blocks & Wires were also acquired by Grimwades, and these were used to show tea cups and saucers to advantage, or sets of jugs, blancmange moulds, teapots and butter dishes. Smaller blocks were used for trios (cup, saucer and tea plate) or samples of dinner ware. Wall mounted hardwood strips were available for displaying wash stand sets.

In 1920, a laboratory was set up at the Victory Works at the Stoke Pottery. This was run under the supervision of Leonard Grimwade's son, Charles Donovan, who had for some years been in charge of a large tile and brick works at Tongshan, North China. Grimwades anticipated cheaper production and improved quality and they tested new methods and new materials 'so that we may be in a strong position for future business'. Also that year, gas fired tunnel ovens were pioneered by Grimwades. These had been laid just after the Armistice and were opened in September 1920. The huge tunnels (298 feet in length) were capable of turning out as much ware as six full-sized ovens.

The railway strike in 1920 affected delivery of goods to customers, so Leonard Grimwade purchased a new 'Karrier' motor lorry for a cost of £1300. This proved so successful – 'No breakage – no delay – no incivility on the part of carters and a lessening of serious inconveniences' – that the company aimed to build up a complete system of motor transport during 1921.

In 1929, a new showroom was set up at Winton House in Stoke-on-Trent. It was named the Victoria Showroom and was to be used for tableware of all kinds, especially bowls, vases and jardinieres. 'It will be used exclusively for representative selections of the latest and most artistic productions', ran the advertisement. It was to be the third showroom at Winton House. The Royal Showroom catered for the dinner ware, toilet ware, teapots and coffee sets and so on, while the Excelsior Showroom was devoted to clearance lines suitable for sales.

Leonard Grimwade died in 1931 with James Plant (Senior) dying in the same year. Plant's son, another James, took over as Managing director in 1933 and he died in 1962.

In January 1964, the company was taken over by the Howard Pottery Co Ltd of Shelton.

Part of Grimwades production (50% of which was exported mainly to Australia, Canada and New Zealand) was moved from Stoke to Norfolk Street, Shelton, with the remainder being transferred some weeks later. The name Royal Winton was kept.

The ware was highly ornamental and much of it was hand painted. There was also a great proportion of gold fancies made, with a specially air conditioned room being set aside for the application of the gold. Orders went out all over the world. Canada formed the largest overseas market, with Australia and New Zealand close behind. A new 'Royal Winton' tie-on label had been designed and this was printed in the Howard colours of chocolate brown, white and grey.

Between 1964 and the present day there have been several successive owners of Royal Winton. Pentagon Holdings acquired Howard Pottery in late 1960, and supplied Taunton Vale Industries with ware. Pentagon itself went on the market in 1973 and was bought by its erstwhile customer, Taunton Vale Industries Ltd. In 1979 the Staffordshire Potteries purchased Taunton Vale Industries and in 1986 were themselves taken over by Coloroll (Ceramics Division). Despite all the various takeovers, the name Royal Winton was kept alive.

When Coloroll was declared bankrupt in 1990/91, there was a management buy-out for Royal Winton. In 1993, the company was purchased by Spencer Hammer Associates and a new company formed: Burnan International Limited.

In 1995 Royal Winton became part of the Taylor Tunnicliffe Group and in October of that year brought back the Grimwade name by registering the company as Grimwades, trading as Royal Winton. Since that time, they have reproduced many of the Chintz patterns.

Leonard L. Grimwade

Leonard Lumsden Grimwade was a man of extraordinary vitality and enthusiasm, and the driving force behind Grimwades Royal Winton Pottery. The *North Staffordshire Echo* profiled him in 1907, describing him as 'quick in all his movements, restless in activity, audacious in projects, with fine imagination and generous sentiments, he is an interesting personality and an admirable ally.'

Lily Bell, who worked at Winton Potteries during the 1920s and 1930s said, "Leonard Grimwade, he was absolutely alive. He was full of it. No sooner than he'd thought anything, he was off – he was like a bottle of pop; got to be doing."

Leonard Grimwade was born in Ipswich in 1864, the youngest of nine children. Large families were then common; Leonard's father, Richard Grimwade (1816-1905), was one of 15 children, while his uncle, Edward, produced 17 children. Leonard's grandfather, William Grimwade (1782-1856), was a Suffolk man who owned Poplar Farm at Wetheringsett, some 16 miles from Ipswich. Amy Langdon, Leonard Grimwade's mother, was a woollen draper at the time of her marriage.

At 16, Leonard moved to Hanley in North Staffordshire where he worked for his uncle, Edward, as a 'dry-salter'. According to a contemporary dictionary, the term dry-salter had two definitions: a dealer in dried and salted meats, pickles and sauces, or a dealer in dye stuffs, chemical products etc. As Leonard's uncle was a chemist, it can be assumed that the boy worked with chemicals rather than pickles.

By 1880, however, he was working as a decorator and modeller in the potteries. He soon began to show signs of the restless energy and dynamism that were to characterise him in later life and, shortly before he was 21, he opened his own business as a factor, the manufacturing side being developed gradually. His first premises consisted of no more than a shed in a yard, sited between two rows of cottages but, before long, he was in a position to invite his elder brother Sidney Richard Grimwade, a potter, to join him in his venture. And so, in 1885, the firm of Grimwade Brothers was founded. Around the late 1880s, another Grimwade brother, Edward Ernest, joined the firm. He was later to represent the company's interests in Australasia, leaving England in 1905 to live in New Zealand.

In 1886, Leonard returned to Ipswich to marry Marion Cooper (1865-1925).There were three children of the marriage: a son, Charles Donovan Grimwade (1890-1971), and two daughters, Elsie (born in 1892) and Muriel (born in 1907). It appeared to have been a happy marriage. The Grimwades celebrated their silver wedding anniversary in style in 1911 when family members, colleagues and employees, (in all numbering some 900 people), filled the Victoria Hall at Hanley. The *Staffordshire Sentinel* reported that the couple had been presented with a gift from their employees of a silver rose bowl and two silver vases.

There was another reason for the celebration, the *Staffordshire Sentinel* declared. 'It was primarily a recognition by the firm of the loyalty of its employees during the rush of orders attendant upon the Coronation.'

Leonard Grimwade's reply to the presentation threw light on his early days as a manufacturer. When he wooed and won his wife all those years ago, he said, the business of Grimwades Ltd was in its infancy. The whole work of the firm was carried on in one small warehouse, and he was the warehouseman, ledger clerk, and sometimes the packer. This statement was greeted with much laughter and applause.

Marion Grimwade died in 1925 and Leonard re-married shortly afterwards. His new wife, Minnie, presented him with a baby girl, Janet, in 1927.

Charles Donovan Grimwade was to follow his father into the pottery business. He left school at 17 and worked at the Shelton laboratory in 1908, later moving to the Atlas works. When he was twenty, he was presented with a bronze medal by the County Borough of Stoke-on-Trent. The inscription reads: *Higher Education Committee. Examination in Pottery. Charles Donovan Grimwade. 2nd Place Honours Grade 1910-11.*

Shortly after taking the examination in 1912, Charles Donovan went to China where he was in charge of the Chinese Mining and Engineering Company. Based in Tongshan, North China, the works was spread over two acres and manufactured tiles and stonework piping as well as bricks. Charles Donovan was responsible for reporting on the state of affairs in clay mining, works machinery and output, as well as estimating the quantities needed, weight and cost, and time of manufacture for articles produced.

He left Tongshan in December 1915 to join the army. He left for Petrograd via the Trans-Siberian Railway, then travelled by sledge to the Swedish railway (in the Arctic winter) then on to Bergen in Norway. He reached England on January 13th 1916 and soon received a commission going first to Egypt, then Palestine, being present at the capture of Jerusalem.

After the war, he became scientific advisor to Grimwades, and was soon on the Board of Directors. He married Nora Gibson in1920, the daughter of Arthur Gibson, who was well-known for his manufacture of teapots. The couple had one daughter, Stella Ruth.

Charles Donovan's work in China appears to have been recognised by his father, as several shape names bear reference to the oriental. The 1918 catalogue, for example, shows a **Tientsin** toilet set and a **Tongshan** vase. The war years were also commemorated in the same catalogue, with toilet ware having shape names such as **Belgium** and **Somme**.

As the silver wedding celebration showed, Leonard Grimwade was known as a kindly employer. In 1892, *The Pottery Gazette* recorded a New Year's Day party at Grimwades. 'In one of the large rooms at the new works, which had been tastefully decorated for the occasion, a sumptuous repast had been spread . . . A lengthy programme of music – vocal and instrumental – readings, dancing and various games, gave pleasure to all.'

Several employees who worked at Royal Winton during the 1930s and earlier mentioned the room resembling a ballroom that was at the top of the building. "It [the ballroom] was massive. There were great wide stairs and a lovely wooden banister," one worker said. "It looked to me as though it had been a place that had had a lot of money spent on it years ago. Upstairs it was very nice. We used to practice [dancing] there in our lunch time." Another worker recalled the sprung maple floor and lamented the day it was turned into a showroom for toilet and dinner ware.

The girls entered into the spirit of Christmas at the factory. Florence Dennis remembers how they made paper decorations. "We decorated the shop with crêpe paper we bought for tuppence a roll. We made orchids on a steel knitting needle and hung them all around, all the loveliest colours. I'll never forget it. And Leonard Grimwade came in and he said, 'Fairyland! It's fairyland. Beautiful.' He walked through in his plus-fours; he was a grand old man."

At the turn of the century, business was booming and the export trade was brisk. The year 1900 saw the acquisition of the Stoke Pottery and Grimwades Ltd was established, while a new showroom was set up in London. Between 1901 and 1907, four more potteries were bought out and added to the Grimwades Group.

In 1906, Grimwades took out a full page advertisement in *The Pottery Gazette* in order to contradict 'Two Representatives of Earthenware Manufacturers in Staffordshire who have persistently published malicious statements to the effect that we are not Manufacturers, but only Decorators or Factors. We have been compelled to take out Legal Proceedings in order to prevent such innuendoes.' The statement went on: 'We are just publishing a little 'brochure' explaining the chief processes carried on in making pottery.'

The brochure was ostensibly printed to commemorate the opening of the new showrooms at Winton Pottery on October 25th 1906, but would have had a secondary purpose of squashing any further talk or rumours. The booklet, entitled *A Short Description of the Art of Potting...as carried on by Grimwades Ltd at Winton, Stoke, Elgin & Upper Hanley Potteries*, is well illustrated with scenes showing the clay presses in the slip house, the potters' shop, the 'biscuit' warehouse and so on. Some of the photographs were later used for a commemorative catalogue issued in 1913.

The company was awarded a gold medal for some of its Hygienic Patented Ware in 1911, at the Festival of Empire, Imperial Exhibition and Pageant.

King George V and Queen Mary visited the Potteries in 1913 and Grimwades issued a catalogue commemorating the royal visit. This gave a short history of the firm as well as illustrating their ware. In addition, photographs (taken from the 1906 booklet) showed interiors of the dinner ware showroom, the toilet ware showroom, warehouses and the mould makers' shop. It also illustrated how employees carried out skills such as plate making, aerographing, gilding and enamelling.

During their visit, the royal couple toured numerous factories before attending an exhibition at the King's Hall in Stoke-on-Trent. *The Pottery Gazette* reported in their June edition that 'Grimwades had the largest individual exhibit in the whole display'.

The company were showing their new 'Jacobean' ware, a vine-leafed pattern which was a copy of early 17th century tapestry. Also featured was **Royal Hampton**, a pattern taken from old Queen Anne chintz, and 'executed in pink, black and green'. **Royal Dorset** was another new pattern and this consisted of massed roses on a black ground.

The Queen was apparently delighted to purchase a Grimwades Winton teaset in the new **Queen Mary Chintz**. She was also pleased to receive a gift of the **Mecca Foot Warmer** (a type of oval ceramic hot water bottle) in the **Jacobean** pattern. Leonard Grimwade, never one to miss a promotional opportunity, later used a full colour illustration of this in a catalogue describing the foot warmer as, 'Graciously accepted by Her Majesty the Queen'. An ornate gold and red crown decorates the head of the page.

Two days later, the exhibition was moved to Harrods' Stores in London and from there it went to the Liverpool Trades Exhibition.

It is sometimes thought that it was at around this period that Royal Winton adopted the prefix Royal to the Winton trade name. In actual fact, the Home Office, whose records go back to 1897, can find no trace of Grimwades applying for, or receiving, permission to use the word 'Royal' as a prefix. However a catalogue for 1896 (when the firm was still trading as Grimwade Brothers) shows a full colour illustration of *Royal Winton Ware*. This shows tea and coffee pots and other tea wares made in plain colours of celadon, terracotta, ivory and beige, banded with contrasting colours of sage green, brown and turquoise blue.

The name Royal Winton does not appear again, however, until 1917/18 and then vanishes again until about 1929 when Grimwades took out a full page advertisement in *The Pottery Gazette* introducing their new **Octron** vegetable dish made in Royal Winton Ivory.

The year 1920 was a year of change. Grimwades purchased a new 5-ton 'Karrier' motor lorry, costing £1300. The company also installed gas-fired tunnel ovens which were to be 'lit-up' in September of that year. The famous *Quick-Cooker* was now being made in aluminium instead of semi-porcelain as before and a research laboratory was erected at the Victory Works (part of the Winton Works) with Charles Donovan Grimwade supervising it.

A catalogue for this period sounds a hopeful note: 'The War has so completely revolutionised industry that we embrace the opportunity which reconstruction offered for the complete reorganisation of our six factories. The introduction of new and approved methods of 'MASS PRODUCTION', whereby orders can be dispatched more promptly and output can be increased, has enabled us to give greater satisfaction to customers and employees alike.'

Grimwades now employed well over a thousand workers and a Managers' Council was set up by the company to form a link between the directors and the staff in order to increase efficiency.

Further care was taken of workers. The 1920 catalogue reports that: 'A charming bungalow at Ashley Heath has, by the kindness of Mr & Mrs L.L. Grimwade, been placed at the disposal of the 'Welfare Work' and any of our workers needing a rest or country air, can have a few days there to recuperate . . . Many have been completely set up and strengthened for the duties of life at this bracing spot. Already the health of our workers has so improved that frequently it is difficult to find even 3 or 4 out of 1,500 employees who need the recreative benefits which this institution provides.'

The Ashley Heath bungalow was the site of a works outing in Easter of that year, when 85 employees sat down to tea and enjoyed sports and games on the heath.

Leonard Grimwade kept his finger on the pulse of his empire, and he travelled extensively, visiting the United States, Canada, Italy, Germany, Switzerland, Norway, Belgium, Holland, Egypt and Australia. Compelled by his restless energy to realise the value of time, he was one of the earliest motorists and drove his own car.

He was a Liberal free-trader and served on the Stoke-on-Trent County Borough Council. He was also a Justice of the Peace for Staffordshire and Secretary of the Potteries Association for the Promotion of Federation. When examined during the passing of the Federation Bill through Parliament he was asked where he lived. "I sleep in Wolstanton," came the reply, "but I live in the Potteries."

Perhaps his words make a fitting epitaph for such a man.

He died as he had lived – at top speed – in a car crash when on his way to the factory on the 26th January 1931. Accompanied by his nephew, who was in the passenger seat, Leonard Grimwade failed to avoid a bus at crossroads. He died almost instantaneously and was buried at Hartshill Cemetery.

A report in *The Pottery Gazette* stated: 'There was a big cortège, representing all sections of the local life of the Potteries, and the floral tributes were eloquent of the sense of loss which, by the passing of Mr Grimwade, the district has sustained.'

Royal Winton Chintz Ware

The term 'chintz' applies to the tightly grouped, small floral patterns which are reminiscent of chintz fabrics, for example, **Marguerite** and **Balmoral**. Sheet transfer printed patterns are not necessarily floral but cover the whole piece with an 'allover' design, such as **Queen Anne** or **Paisley**. Both chintz and sheet pattern wares are popular with collectors today.

Grimwades first introduced chintz patterns in 1913, with ware decorated in **Hampton** Chintz, **Spode** Chintz, **Ribbon** Chintz and the **Jacobean** pattern. These were sheet transfer printed patterns, the flowers being large or widely spaced. The first closely packed sheet pattern was used in 1923 when **Paisley** was made. In 1928, the chintz ware that is collected today made its first appearance with the **Marguerite** pattern. This was based on the design of a cushion cover that Minnie Grimwade (Leonard Grimwade's second wife) was embroidering at the time.

In 1931, **Delphinium** chintz was produced, and that was followed in 1932 by **Summertime**.

It would appear, from regular reports in *The Pottery Gazette,* that Royal Winton was the leader in the field of chintz ware, easily outstripping manufacturers such as James Kent, Crown Ducal, W.R. Midwinter, and Elijah Cotton who made Nelson Ware.

Leonard Grimwade had bought a large number of shares in the Chromo Transfer and Potters' Supply Co Ltd in 1908 and he was able to translate his ideas for patterns quickly into the reality of transfer printed sheets. He was enthusiastic about the new chintz and, according to Lily Bell who worked at Winton Potteries at the time, he 'would rush out of his office if he saw a girl with a nice overall [a type of wrap-around pinafore] on, like a chintzy pattern, and get her on one side and ask her to leave her overall behind [when she went home] and get someone to take a drawing of it. It'd be a pattern in no time.'

As Leonard Grimwade died in 1931, a great many patterns must already have been in the production pipeline at the time of his death.

The two men who actually put the new patterns down on paper were Mr E.E. Parry, Art Director, and Gilbert Sergeant, Decorating Manager. Between them, they produced innumerable patterns. Florence Dennis, who was also employed by Grimwades during that period recalled, 'There were umpteen patterns in chintz – and Bert Sergeant did quite a lot of designing.'

Chintz patterns were applied by means of a lithographic process. First of all, the biscuit (unglazed) ware was dipped into a transparent liquid glaze and then allowed to dry for 24 hours before being fired. The backstamp was rubber stamped on to the ware before glazing, the glaze being transparent. Once dry the ware was fired in a kiln, allowed to cool and then collected by the girls who were to do the decorating.

The transfer sheets were supplied by the Chromo-Transfer and Potters' Supply Co Ltd who were based at the Winton Potteries. Albert Stevenson, who worked at Winton Potteries for over 30 years said, "The sheets of transfers were hung on a line to dry, rather like washing. The girls, called transferrers or lithographers would cut off the required amount needed and take it back to their bench."

Lithographing was hard work. Glue, (called *size*) was brushed on to the ware by means of a camel hair brush and left to become tacky. Glazed ware, rather than biscuit, was used for chintz as this gave the finished article brighter colours. Unfortunately, this brightness was sometimes at the cost of the durability of the pattern. The lithographer would then cut the sheet of transfer to fit the object as nearly as possible, using a pair of long pointed scissors. Florence Dennis commented, "It was very intricate. We didn't have knives like we had later, where you could nick around the spout of the teapot, for example. But it was very interesting, and I loved it. The harder the pattern, the better I liked it, because I've done nothing else all my life, only lithograph."

The cut pieces of transfer were pressed onto the sized ware. Mrs Dennis explained, "Then I fetched a pot of boiling water from the geyser and took it to the bench. You rubbed with a hard sponge, then a soft one, to take the paper off (leaving the transfer printed pattern adhering to the sized surface). Then you went over it with a clean rag."

To avoid an obvious join, the flowers were often cut into one another, although some badly mis-matched work can be found. Seams and creases were frowned upon and mistakes were not tolerated.

The pattern name was also put on at this stage and the girls often marked their work with a small gilded or painted mark. These marks were put on to the base of the piece, so that any poor or unacceptable work could be traced to the culprit. Sybil Stevenson, for example, used three small dots set in a triangle, rather like two eyes and a nose, to mark her work.

If the work was so bad that even touching up by a skilled paintress was impossible, then the lithographer responsible had to remove the transfer. This was done by soaking the piece in a bucket of soda water, then laboriously scraping off the transfer. As the girls were paid on a piece work basis for finished work, their mistakes could cost them dearly.

Girls were trained initially to decorate a cup (both inside and out) and a saucer, and the completed article had to be passed by an inspector to prove the girl's worth as a lithographer.

After adding any gilding necessary to the piece, it was again fired in the kiln in order to fuse the colours into the glaze and so make them almost permanent. The colours of prefired pieces were 'dull but, after firing, they came up nice and bright.'

Some of the chintz designs were reserved exclusively for the Winton Potteries, but a few were sold to other pottery manufacturers, especially during the 1950s. **Rose du Barry** for example, has been seen on ware produced by several other companies; however, the piece illustrated on page 68 bears the Royal Winton backstamp. **Paisley**, too, was used by others and has been seen in both the rust and blue colourway.

During World War II, the decorating of white ware was forbidden by the government and only practical ware was manufactured. Some unscrupulous dealers would buy up the seconds, then approach factory girls, paying them good money to decorate a teaset or other items in chintz.

One worker admitted, "I did the black market work. This bloke came to the door and asked me to do him 10 china tea sets – he had a couple of sheets of litho, maybe two or three sheets. And I said 'Yes, I'll get you something out of these'.'

She was paid half a crown (12½ pence) per teaset which she thought was marvellous. "We had bad times in the potteries then," she said. "So I did these tea sets and it got a bit more, a bit too much. I realised something was going on. It was in the War, you see."

After the post-war boom, the pottery trade went into recession and, by the early to mid-1950s, chintz ware was no longer being produced. The company was left with a stock of lithographed sheets which were sold on to other manufacturers, and consequently, collectors may find pieces with Royal Winton transfers on products from other potteries.

Royal Winton Shapes

The name of the shape was often impressed in the base of the piece and this has proved helpful to collectors, but as post 1930 catalogues for Royal Winton wares seem to be non-existent, it has not been possible to identify all the shapes. Often, the shape name applied only to single items in the following list, although it is almost certain that other items were also made in the same shape. However, for accuracy, only known items are identified.

Sources and references are given wherever possible. If a shape is illustrated in the book, then an example of the pattern in that shape will be given.

If no illustration for a shape exists, then as full a description as possible will be given. This is not always practical, however, as some shapes are mentioned in catalogues and *The Pottery Gazette* but without illustration.

Shape Names	Product	Pattern illustrated
Ajax	Tea ware	No illustration

This shape was illustrated in a 1930s Grimwades catalogue, and was shown as a fluted 8 or 10-sided cup and 10-sided saucer in both a 'tall' shape (with straight-sided body and a high pointed handle) and a 'low' shape which had straight-sided body tapering sharply to the foot and having an uplifted, squared-off handle, rather like Hastings. The teapot appears to be octagonal, having a squared-off handle and an open rectangular handle to the teapot lid.

Ascot	Cream jug	Esther, 'Blue Tulip'
(Shape No. 970)	Plate: large	Balmoral
	: sandwich	Victorian Rose
	: tea	Queen Anne
	Preserve pot	Cheadle, Royalty
	Sugar bowl	Pekin, Spring
	Sweet dish	Pelham
	Teapot	Hazel

The tea ware was advertised with a full page illustration in *The Pottery Gazette* in November 1932. The pattern shown was Cherry Blossom, a non-chintz design.
Note: Ascot can easily be confused with Athena. For an example, compare the base of the teapots in the Hazel illustration. The base of the Ascot teapot is flat and straight while the base of the Athena teapot is indented, giving the impression of small feet.

Athena	Bowl, 6 sizes	No illustration
	Sweet dish	Clyde
	Teapot	Sweet Pea, Hazel

The bowl was mentioned in a Grimwades catalogue in 1930. No description was given. The tea ware was advertised with a full page illustration in *The Pottery Gazette* in September 1934.
Note: *See Ascot*

Burke	Powder Box	No illustration

Queen Mary purchased a powder box in this shape in the Royalty pattern in February 1937. The Grimwades catalogue for 1923 shows this to be of round, squat, bulbous appearance, widening towards the base. The overlapping lid had no finial or handle with which to lift it.

Cambridge	Jug, squarish	No illustration
Candy Box	Rectangular box	Queen Anne

The words CANDY BOX are impressed on the base of this piece. A catalogue for 1930 shows this listed as an 'Oblong' Box.

Chelsea   Preserve pot   No illustration

The preserve pot is of globular form and has a round lid with a squarish knob. The separate stand is also round.

Chrysta   Powder Box   No illustration

A Grimwades invoice shows that Queen Mary purchased a powder box in this shape in the Royalty pattern in February 1937. No description was given.

Cintra   Flower vase   Cheadle

Countess   Covered sugar bowl   Cromer
                     Jug, various sizes   Fireglow (Black)
                     Teapot   Pekin

Note: The shape of the jug can easily be confused with that of Globe. However, careful comparison will show that the pouring lip of Countess is narrower and slightly more upward pointing than that of Globe.

Crown   Bowl 6½", 8" and 9" sizes   Marguerite catalogue illustration

Dane   Biscuit barrel with wicker handle   No illustration
                     Bowl 5"   Florette catalogue illustration
                     Cheese dish   'Rose Spray' and Richmond

A cheese dish in the Dane shape was first produced in 1913. The open rectangular handle was ornately moulded but in the 1930s and onwards, a plain, simple handle was also available. Richmond has an ornate handle; 'Rose Spray' is plain. A Grimwades catalogue for 1922 shows the biscuit barrel to be of rounded form tapering to a footed base. The top is indented at the handles, flaring out to the rim with a round knob on the lid.

Delamere   Stacking set of teapot,   Sunshine
                     cream and sugar

Delius   Jug/ewer   No illustration

A tall handled jug or ewer having a bulbous base and going in at the 'waist' before widening briefly and narrowing again. The jug then flares widely at the top.

Duchess   Teapot   No illustration

A teapot in the Duchess shape was purchased by Queen Mary in February 1937. No pattern name was shown on the Grimwades invoice, only the pattern number 3030. Duchess dinner ware was illustrated in a Grimwades catalogue for 1925/28. However, no illustration was shown for tea ware.

Dutch   Jug, various sizes   Kinver

This shape was first mentioned in a catalogue dated 1923.

Duval   Jug, 3 sizes   Florette and Marguerite catalogue illustrations

Elite   Jug stand   Marguerite catalogue illustration
                     Teapot (3 sizes)   Florette and Marguerite catalogue illustrations

This shape was first illustrated in a Grimwades catalogue dated 1923 when it featured an Elite cream jug in the Paisley pattern. The shape is round and globular – a rounder and flatter version of the Globe jug. The teapot is also round and globular, with a strawberry finial to the lid.

Era   Mint boat/stand   Florence

Etona   Vase   No illustration

Of tubular form, the vase is wider at the base than the top. It curves gently inward to about half its height, then curves outward slightly.

Fife   Bowl   No illustration
                     Roll tray   Florette catalogue illustration
                     Sandwich tray   Floral Feast

A Fife Bowl No. 1 in the Queen Anne pattern was purchased by Queen Mary on the 15th July 1937. The bowls were made in various sizes. Fife supper sets, consisting of a slightly dished tray with six small tea plates, were illustrated in a Grimwades catalogue for 1930.

Gem   Rose bowl   No illustration

A round globular bowl with a short stem and wide foot. It was fitted with a brass grid-like top to hold the roses in place.

Globe	Jug, 4 sizes	Crocus, Peony
	Sugar bowl	Majestic, Peony
	Teapot, 3 sizes; Teapot stand	No illustration

The teapot first went into production in 1896 and is known to have been made, still in the same shape, until at least 1925/28. The teapot is round and globular with a slight foot rim. The lid sits snugly inside the collar of the pot and has a mushroom shaped knob or finial. It is not known whether or not it was made in chintz patterns.

Note: The shape of the jug can easily be confused with that of Countess. Careful examination will show that the pouring lip of Globe is wider and more shallow than that of Countess.

Gordon	Candy dish	No illustration

No description is available, other than the lid or cover has a pointed top.

Grecian	Cream jug	Spring

Greek	Coffee pot 1¼ pint	'Paisley'
	Jug stand	No illustration

The Greek shape, introduced in 1918 was used on various items of tableware, including salad bowls, biscuit jars, honey pots (with fast stands) and lids etc. The coffee pot shape of this period more resembled a hot water jug, its spout more of a large pouring lip; it was later modified to the shape shown in 'Paisley'.

Grosvenor	Posy bowl	No illustration

A hexagonal globular bowl, the top being of a slightly larger diameter than the base.

Hampton	Basket	Clevedon

First shown in a Grimwades catalogue dated 1930.

Hastings	Cup and saucer	Beeston, Rutland

Hector	Sugar bowl	Kinver

Hurstmere	Sugar bowl, 3¼"	Marguerite catalogue illustration

Imperial	Coffee cup/saucer	Florette catalogue illustration

Jacobean	Tea ware	No illustration

A cream and sugar set (private collection) show the jug has a sharply angular handle, similar to Hastings. The piece narrows towards the base in three 'steps'.

King	Cup and saucer	Cheadle, Welbeck
	Salad bowl	No illustration

A salad bowl and servers No 2 and No 2A, Sweet Pea pattern, was sold to Queen Mary on the 15th July 1936.

Lotus *See Octron*

Mecca	Foot warmer	Marguerite

Muffin	Covered muffin	Marguerite

Musical Box	Rectangular box	Marion

Nita	Wall pocket	No illustration

This is of an in-curving, elongated tulip shape, narrowing at the base to a small knob. There are two scrolling 'handles' halfway down each side of the pocket. The open top is formed by three arcs, the centre curve being wider than the two flanking arcs. Could possibly be described as a fleur-de-lys shape.

Norman	Teapot	Chintz

Tea ware in this shape was illustrated in the Buyers' Notes section of *The Pottery Gazette* in July 1932, with a full page advertisement for Beverley patterned dinner ware (a non-chintz pattern) shown in the same publication in December 1932.

Octavius	Bowl (8-sided)	Florette catalogue illustration
	Bon bon or chocolate comport	No illustration

The comport was mentioned in a 1930s catalogue price list, when it sold for 19/6 (97½ pence) per dozen.

Octron Plate Fireglow (White)
Sweet dish (8-sided) Florette catalogue illustration

The plate has ten sides despite the shape name which would indicate an 8-sided shape, but reference to a Grimwade catalogue for 1930 confirms this rather odd anomaly. There appears to be no dictionary definition of the word Octron. The same sweet dish is shown in the Marguerite catalogue illustration under the name of Lotus. This was a misprint and was corrected in the price list in the same catalogue.

Orleans Plate, large Somerset

The catalogue for 1925/28 shows that a rectangular Orleans sandwich plate, together with six square tea plates, was sold as a sandwich or supper set.

Remus Large vase/jug Hazel

Rex Triple tray Illustration of Pattern number 4252
Cheese dish 3 sizes: No. 1, 2 and 2a Marguerite catalogue illustration

The Rex cheese dish was introduced in 1913 when it had a slightly fluted body. Later cheese dishes from the 1930s period kept the same general shape but had a more squared-off body.

Rheims Salad bowl with chromed rim Somerset
Biscuit barrel White Rose

The biscuit barrel is also shown in the Marguerite catalogue illustration (at the bottom left hand corner of the picture) with a slightly different knob to the lid.

Rosa Wall pocket No illustration

A double wall pocket of elongated triangular shape ending in a curved point. The pockets appear to overlap each other in a stepped manner and are enhanced by the addition of 3 semicircular 'ears' on one side of the pocket.

Rowsley Basket No illustration

The handled basket has a wavy rim and flares from the footed base in a high sided gondola shape.

Ryde Ashtray No illustration

A rectangular ashtray of Art Deco form with an irregular, stepped interior.

Shell Butter/jam dish No illustration

This small dish is shaped and fluted rather like a cockle shell.

Stafford Fruit bowl Marguerite catalogue illustration
Long tray Marguerite catalogue illustration
Watercress dish and stand No illustration

A Stafford tea cup, illustrated in a Grimwades catalogue for 1930, shows a wide cup tapering to the base with a sharp inward indentation to the foot. The squarish handle is slightly upward pointing. The water cress dish and stand was first mentioned in a price list for 1925/28 and then cost 3/6d (17½ p). Dinner ware also appeared in the same catalogue.

Stella Fruit set with a 9" bowl Marguerite catalogue illustration

Tennis Set Cup with matching saucer/plate Mayfair, 'Gold Leaves'

Queen Mary purchased 6 tennis sets in pattern 4808 at a cost of 1 shilling (5p) each in February 1939. The tennis set in the "Gold Leaves" pattern is larger than usual.

Troy Fruit bowl square 9" Marguerite catalogue illustration
(lower half of the page)

Tea ware in the Troy shape was also made c1925/28 for Atlas China, a factory which was part of the Grimwades group.

Trefoil Butter pat dish Wild Flowers

Tudor Vase No illustration

A vase of tubular tapering form, narrowing from the top to a wide base.

Vera Cream jug Marguerite

Winton Cream jug 2oz, 'Exotic Bird' and Marguerite
4oz, 8oz,10oz. catalogue illustration

The Winton shape first went into production in 1922.

BARKER BROTHERS

Barker Brothers, **Blue Chintz** dessert dish (£40-£50/ $70-$100).

Barker Brothers, **Butterflies** large platter 11" diameter, (£70-£80/$125-$155).

Barker Brothers, **Hydrangea** large platter 11" diameter, (£75-£80/$130-$155).

Barker Brothers, **Lorna Doone** triple cakestand (£60-£70/$105-$135).

Barker Brother 6-cup teapot with unknown pattern and shape (£250-£300/$440-$585).

Barker Brothers, **Peonies & Chrysanthemums**, large fruit bowl (£80-£100/$140-$195).

BARKER BROTHERS

ELIJAH COTTON (Lord Nelson)

Barker Brothers, **Trellis Roses**, large, shaped tea plate (£75-£80/$130-$155).

Booths Ltd, **Evesham** sugar bowl (£50-£60/$90-$115).

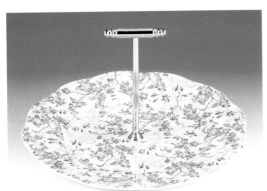

British Anchor Pottery, **Apple Blossom** 9" diameter cake plate, (£35-£45/$60-$90).

Burgess Brothers, **Daisies**, (£40-£50/$70-$100).

Chapman's Longton Virginia Stock, Trio (£40-£50/$70-$100); 5" diameter shaped dish (£30-£40/$55-$80).

Elijah Cotton Anemone stacking teapot, cream jug and sugar bowl (£350-£425/$615-$830).

ELIJAH COTTON (Lord Nelson)

Elijah Cotton **Black Beauty** cup and saucer in Art Deco shape (£60-£70/$105-$135).

Elijah Cotton **Black Beauty** tea plate (£35-£45/$60-$90).

Elijah Cotton **Briar Rose** plate, (£30-£40/$55-$80).

Elijah Cotton Green Tulip, shaped tea plate (£55-£65/$95-$125).

Elijah Cotton Heather Octagonal cake plate, (£40-£45/$70-$90).

Elijah Cotton **Marina**, shaped tea plate (£40-£50/$70-$100).

Elijah Cotton **Pansy** pierced handle dish, 7" x 5½", £70-£80/$125-$155.

19

ELIJAH COTTON (Lord Nelson)

Elijah Cotton Pansy 11¾" diameter with relief moulded border (£120-£150/$210-$295).

Elijah Cotton **Rosetime** dish (£80-£90/$140-$175).

Elijah Cotton **Rosetime** 8⅜" plate (£80-£90/$140-$175).

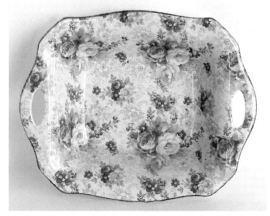

Elijah Cotton **Rosetime** dish (£100-£120/$175-$235).

Elijah Cotton **Rosetime** dish (£70-£80/$125-$155).

Elijah Cotton **Royal Brocade** 6" oblong dish (£70-£80/ $125-$155).

ELIJAH COTTON (Lord Nelson)   EMPIRE PORCELAIN

*Elijah Cotton **Skylark** plate, (£60-£75/$105-$145).*

Deans Delton Ware fruit bowl, (£80-£90/$140-$175).

Deans Lucerne Ware fruit bowl, (£80-£90/$140-$175).

*Empire Porcelain Co **Black Marguerite** oval fluted dish (£70-£80/$125-$155).*

*Empire Porcelain Co **Golden Wattle** 2-pint milk jug (£90-£100/$160-$195).*

*Empire Porcelain Co **Lilac Time** covered sugar bowl (£60-£70/$105-$135).*

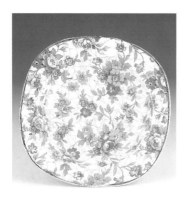

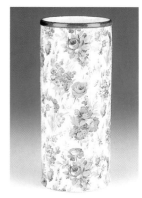

*Empire Porcelaine Co **Rosalie** tea plate (£40-£50/$70-$100).*

*Empire Porcelain Co **Water Lily** square cake plate (£55-£60/$95-$115).*

*T. G. Green **Harmony** (£60-£70/ $105-$135).*

*Royal Winton **Anemone**: A large bread and butter plate (£85-£100/$150-$195) with an Art Deco diamond-shaped dish (£60-£70/$105-$135).*

*Royal Winton **Beauvais**: A large jardiniere in the **Argyle** shape, (£300-£350/$525-$685).*

*Royal Winton **Bedale**: An un-footed fruit bowl in the **Stafford** shape (£400-£500/$700-$980).*

*Royal Winton **Beeston**: Art Deco trio of cup, saucer and plate in the **Hastings** shape (£120-£150/$210-$295).*

GRIMWADES (Royal Winton)

Royal Winton Balmoral: Bedside set, (£1100-£1200/$1925-$2350).

*Royal Winton Balmoral: An **Ascot** shape bread and butter plate (£90-£115/$160-$225), a small **Countess** teapot (£250-£300/$440-$585), and a shaped, rectangular sweet dish (£70-£80/$125-$155).*

GRIMWADES (Royal Winton)

Royal Winton Beeston: **Ascot** shape teapot with teapot stand (£750-£950/ $1315-$1860).

Royal Winton **Birds and Tulips**: a wide, angular cup and saucer in the Art Deco style, edged with gilding, (£60-£80/$105-$155).

Royal Winton 'Black Daisies': A rectangular fruit with shaped ends (£70-£80/$125-$155).

Royal Winton Blackberries: A **Globe** shaped jug (£90-£100/$160-$195).

Royal Winton 'Blocked Roses': An **Ascot** cake plate (£50-£60/$90-$115).

Royal Winton Blue Jade: A small **Countess** milk jug (£60-£80/$105-$155).

GRIMWADES (Royal Winton)

*Royal Winton Blue Tulip: A cream jug in the **Ascot** shape £60-£70/$105-$135) and a coffee can and saucer (£65-£75/$115-$145).*

Royal Winton Carnation (£35-£40/$60-$80).

*Royal Winton Cheadle: A flower vase in **Cintra** shape (£200-£220/$350-$430), a large **Countess** teapot, (£500-£600/$875-$1175), a footed bon-bon dish (up-ended), (£160-£180/$280-$350), a preserve pot with matching lid and stand in the **Ascot** shape (£180-£220/$315-$430) and a cup and saucer (£75-£85/$130-$165).*

GRIMWADES (Royal Winton)

Royal Winton Cheadle teapot and stand (£750-£850/ $1315-$1665) on **Alban** with **Chelsea** jam pot (£140-£160/$245-$315); plate (£65-£75/$115-$145); tea cup and saucer (£75-£85/$130-$165).

Royal Winton Chelsea: A hot water jug (£750-£850/ $1315-$1595) and a large bread and butter plate (£120-£150/$210-$295) in the **Ascot** shape.

Royal Winton Chelsea Globe shape jugs (£100-£150/ $175-$295); (£180-£240/$315-$470); and (£270-£320/ $475-$625).

Royal Winton Chintz: An Art Deco teapot in the **Norman** shape (£150-£200/$265-$390).

Royal Winton Clevedon: A fluted oval dish (£90-£100/ $160-$195), a small basket (£300-£350/$525-$685) in the **Hampton** shape and a footed bon–bon dish (£250-£300/$440-$585).

Royal Winton Clyde: An **Ascot** bread and butter plate (£60-£70/$105-$135), an oblong sweet dish in the **Athena** shape (£60-£70/$105-$135) and a tennis set (£65-£75/$115-$145).

GRIMWADES (Royal Winton)

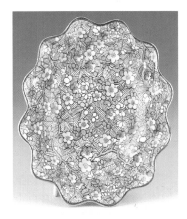

*Royal Winton **Cobwebs**: Sweetmeat dish with crimped edges (£70-£80/$125-$155).*

*Royal Winton **Cotswold**: Bedside set (£850-£900/$1490-$1760).*

*Royal Winton **Cotswold**: a round tea plate (£50-£60/$90-$115).*

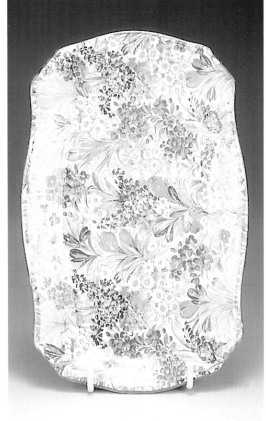

*Royal Winton **Cranstone**: A cup and saucer, (£90-£100/$160-$195).*

*Royal Winton **Crocus** (White): A small oblong sandwich plate in the **Ascot** shape, (£80-£90/$140-$175).*

GRIMWADES (Royal Winton)

Royal Winton Cromer: A covered 2-handled sugar bowl in the **Countess** shape (£70-£90/$125-$175) and an angular **Hastings** shape cup & saucer (£75-£80/$130-$155).

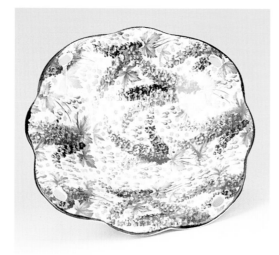

Royal Winton Delphinium Chintz: An up-ended footed comport, (£160-£180/$280-$350).

Royal Winton Dorset: Coffee pot (£250-£300/$440-$585).

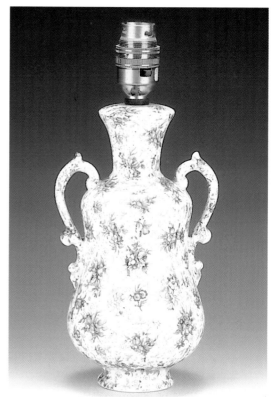

Royal Winton Eleanor: Coffee set (£650-£750/$1140-$1470).

Royal Winton Eleanor: A 2-handled lamp base (£450-£650/$790-$1275).

GRIMWADES (Royal Winton)

Royal Winton English Rose: Tea plate (£50-£60/$90-$115).

Royal Winton Estelle: Tea plate (£45-£50/$80-$100).

Royal Winton Esther: An oblong sandwich tray with shaped ends (£100-£120/$175-$235) and an **Ascot** cream jug (£80-£90/$140-$175).

Royal Winton Esther plate (£80-£100/$140-$195), tea cup and saucer (£80-£90/$140-$175).

GRIMWADES (Royal Winton)

Royal Winton Evesham Bedside: Coffee set (£1600-£1800/$2800-$3525), bedside set (£1500-£1800/$2625-$3525), plate (£75-£85/$130-$165), tea cup and saucer (£90-£100/$160-$195), 3-tier cakestand (£100-£150/$175-$295).

*Royal Winton Evesham: Coffee pot in **Alban shape** (£900-£1000/$1575-$1960).*

Royal Winton Evesham: Bedside set (£1500-£1800/$2625-$3525).

Royal Winton Evesham: A large round teapot (£850-£950/$1490-$1860), a tennis set (£120-£150/$210-$295) and a handled beaker or mug (£250-£300/$440-$585).

*Royal Winton Exotic Bird: A large jug in the **Dutch** shape (£70-£80/$125-$155) and a **Winton** shape cream jug (£60-£70/$105-$135).*

Royal Winton Fernese: An oblong sweet dish in the Art Deco style (£60-£70/$105-$135).

GRIMWADES (Royal Winton)

Royal Winton 'Fibre Roses': Sardine box in the **Greek** *shape, (£60-£100/$105-$195).*

Royal Winton Fireglow (Black): A small square sweet dish (£50-£60/$90-$115), a large oval dish and a **Countess** *jug (£70-£80/$125-$155).*

Royal Winton Fireglow (White) **Sexta** *hot water pot (£350-£450/$615-$880).*

Royal Winton Fireglow (White): A ten-sided cheese plate in the **Octron** *shape (£70-£90/$125-$175).*

Royal Winton Fireglow (White) Bowl (£120-£150/$210-$295).

Royal Winton Floral Feast: A long, deep dished roll tray with open work handles in the **Fife** *shape (£160-£180/$280-$350).*

GRIMWADES (Royal Winton)

Royal Winton Tea and coffee pot collection.

Royal Winton Florence bedside set (£1500-£1800/$2625-$3525).

Royal Winton Florence: A cheese dish in the **Dane** shape with a plain handle (£250-£280/$440-$550), a footed comport (£180-£220/$315-$430) and a mint boat and stand (£150-£180/$265-$350), and nut dish (£70-£80/$125-$155) in the **Era** shape.

Royal Winton Floral Garden: A square sweet dish with shaped 'handles' in the green colourway (£50-£60/$90-$115), an oval 3-sectioned hors d'oeuvre dish in white (£50-£60/$90-$115) and a small butter dish in the **Trefoil** shape in the blue colourway (£50-£60/$90-$115).

Royal Winton Florette: Salad bowl with chromium plated rim (£90-£100/$160-$195).

Royal Winton Gold Leaves: Cream ground tennis set of a size which is larger than usual (£40-£50/$70-$100).

GRIMWADES (Royal Winton)

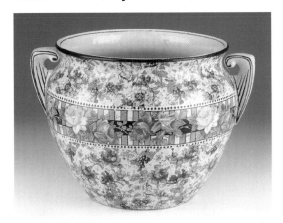

Royal Winton 'Grapes and Roses': A jardiniere in the **Niobe** shape (£250-£350/$440-$685).

Royal Winton Hampton Chintz: Dessert plate in the **Octagon** shape (£40-£50/$70-$100).

Royal Winton Hazel: A jug/flower vase in the **Remus** shape (£850-£950/$1490-$1860), a jardiniere (£800-£950/$1400-$1860), an **Athena** teapot (£550-£600/$965-$1175) and a smaller **Ascot** teapot (£500-£600/$875-$1175).

Royal Winton Hazel: **Ascot** coffee pot (£600-£700/$1050-$1370), and teapot with on stand (£650-£750/$1140-$1470).

Royal Winton Jacobean: Chamber pot in the **Octagon** shape (£250-£300/$440-$585).

Royal Winton Joyce-Lynn: A large breakfast trio comprising a cup, saucer and plate (£75-£85/$130-$165).

GRIMWADES (Royal Winton)

A selection of Royal Winton and Crown Ducal Chintz

Royal Winton Julia: A 2-handled sweet dish (£100-£120/$175-$235), a 3-piece cruet with chromed tops (£180-£200/$315-$390), a handled beaker or mug (£250-£300/$440-$585), a tennis set (£350-£400/$615-$785) and a covered butter dish (£200-£250/$350-$490).

GRIMWADES (Royal Winton)

*Royal Winton Julia: A set of jugs in the **Globe** shape (£65-£120/ $115-$235).*

Royal Winton Julia bedside set (£1100-£1300/$1925-$2275).

Royal Winton Julia Bedside set form two (£1800-£2000/$3150-$3915).

*Royal Winton Julia: **Alban** teapot with stand (£1200-£1500/$2100-$2935), coffee pot (£1200-£1500/$2100-$2935) and Rosebud basket (£600-£650/$1050-$1275).*

Royal Winton June Festival: A large round plate (£40-£50/$70-$100); a hand painted mint boat stand (£25-£35/$45-$70).

GRIMWADES (Royal Winton)

Royal Winton June Roses: An **Ascot** cake plate on a chromed stand (£70-£80/$125-$155).

Royal Winton June Roses: **Ascot** shaped teapot, (£600-£700/$1050-$1370); English Rose on **Albans** shape coffee pot (£600-£700/$1050-$1370).

Royal Winton Kew: A mint boat stand in blue (£60-£80/$105-$155) and a tea plate (£75-£85/$130-$145).

Royal Winton Majestic: **Athena** lidded hot water pot (£750-£850/$1315-$1665).

Royal Winton Kinver: A large jug in the **Dutch** shape (£150-£180/$265-$350) and a small hexagonal sugar in the **Hector** shape (£70-£85/$125-$165).

Royal Winton Majestic: A small deep sweetmeat dish with shaped ends (£95-£115/$165-$225) and a **Globe** sugar bowl (£85-£95/$150-$185).

GRIMWADES (Royal Winton)

Royal Winton Marion: A Musical box (£180-£200/$315-$390).

Royal Winton Mayfair: A tennis set (£100-£120/$175-$235) and a large Tea plate (£80-£90/$140-$175).

Royal Winton May Festival: A round tea plate (£45-£55/$80-$110); a covered butter dish (£85-£95/$150-$185).

Royal Winton Marguerite: A Mecca foot warmer, first introduced in 1913 (£180-£200/$315-$390).

Royal Winton Mayfair: **Malta** shape tray (£95-£115/$165-$225), **Chelsea** shape jam pot (£140-£160/$245-$315), **Albans** shape coffee pot (£650-£750/$1140-$1470), **Ascot** shape pepper, salt, mustard (£180-£200/$315-$390).

GRIMWADES (Royal Winton)

Royal Winton **Merton**: A 2- handled **Orleans** dessert dish (£90-£100/ $160-$195).

Royal Winton **Morning Glory**: A large bread and butter plate in the **Ascot** shape (£60-£70/$105-$135).

Above: Royal Winton Nantwich: Coffee pot in Albans shape (£400-£500/$700-$980).

*Above: Royal Winton Nantwich: An **Ascot** bread and butter plate (£100-£120/$175-$235), a coffee pot (£400-£500/$700-$980), open sugar bowl (£80-£100/$140-$195), a cream jug (£80-£100/ $140-$195) and a coffee cup and saucer (£80-£100/$140-$195).*

*Left: Royal Winton **Old Cottage Chintz**: A round tea plate (£60-£70/$105-$135) and a double egg cup (£160-£180/$280-$350), used for both duck and hen's eggs.*

GRIMWADES (Royal Winton)

Royal Winton **Orient**: A long ribbed dish of Art Deco style (£75-£85/$130-$165).

Royal Winton **Oriental Fantasy**: A sandwich tray in the **Ascot** shape (£50-£60/$90-$115).

Royal Winton **Paisley**: A coffee pot in the **Greek** shape (£80-£100/$140-$195), and a green colourway sandwich tray in the **Ascot** shape (£45-£50/$80-$100).

Paisley: The coffee pot in the blue colourway shows an identical pattern, but was not made by Royal Winton (£80-£100/$140-$195).

Royal Winton **Pebbles**: A footed bon-bon dish (£40-£50/$70-$100).

Royal Winton **Pelham**: A small sweet dish in the **Ascot** shape (£40-£50/$70-$100).

GRIMWADES (Royal Winton)

*Royal Winton Pekin: A small, red hand painted plate (£50-£60/$90-$115), a blue pin tray (backstamp 10) (£30-£40/$55-$80), a black **Countess** teapot (£70-£80/$125-$155) and a cream coffee cup and saucer (£40-£50/$70-$100).*

*Royal Winton Peony: An up-ended **Globe** sugar bowl (£30-£40/$55-$80) and a small **Globe** jug (£45-£55/$80-$110).*

*Royal Winton **Queen Anne**: A tea plate in the **Ascot** shape (£35-£45/$60-$90) and a candy box (impressed CANDY BOX) (£80-£100/$140-$195).*

*Royal Winton **Queen Mary Chintz**: Tête-à-tête set in the **Etna** shape, £100-£150/$175-$295.*

Royal Winton Quilt: A small oval dish (£50-£60/$90-$115) and a sugar sifter (£150-£180/$265-$350).

GRIMWADES (Royal Winton)

Royal Winton Richmond: Cheese dish in the **Dane** shape with an ornate handle (£75-£130/$130-$255). The cheese dish was available in 3 sizes.

Royal Winton Ripon: Small sweet dish (£35-£45/$60-$90) and one of a pair of vases in **Ming** shape (£100-£120/$175-$235).

Royal Winton Rose du Barry: A three-piece cruet on a **Trefoil** shaped stand (£130-£150/$230-$295).

Royal Winton Rose Spray: Cheese dish in the **Dane** shape, available in 3 sizes. The example shown has a plain handle (£90-£100/$160-$195).

Royal Winton Rose Sprig: A canoe-shaped long dish (£55-£65/$95-$125).

Royal Winton 'Rosebuds': Fruit dish in the **Holborn** shape (£45-£55/$80-$110).

GRIMWADES (Royal Winton)

Royal Winton 'Roses': Large trinket tray, **Kensington** shape (£55-£65/$95-$125).

Royal Winton **Royalty**: A chamberstick (£150-£170/$265-$335) and a jam or preserve pot with matching lid and base in the **Ascot** shape (£180-£200/$315-$390).

Royal Winton Royalty: **Athena** teapot (£600-£700/$1050-$1370).

Royal Winton **Royalty**: Plate (£100-£120/$175-$235), Kew Coffee pot (£500-£600/$875-$1175), Beeston teapot and jam pots (£750-£850/$1315-$1665).

Royal Winton Rutland: An angular Art Deco cup and saucer in the **Hastings** shape (£80-£90/$140-$175).

Royal Winton **Sampler**: A beaker, (£90-£100/$160-$195).

GRIMWADES (Royal Winton)

Royal Winton Shrewsbury: **Ascot** cake plate (£130-£150/$230-$295) and a round tea plate (£75-£85/$130-$165).

Royal Winton Somerset: Bedside (£1000-£1200/$1750-$2350).

Royal Winton Somerset: A large cake plate in the **Orleans** shape (£120-£150/$210-$295), a salad bowl with a silver plated rim in the **Rheims** shape (£160-£180/$280-$350) and a bedside set comprising a **Countess** teapot, a cup, a cream jug, an open sugar bowl and a toast rack (£1500-£1800/$2625-$3525).

Royal Winton Spring: An **Ascot** cream jug and sugar bowl (£150-£160/$265-$315), a cream jug in the **Grecian** shape (shown standing on a wooden block) (£100-£120/$175-$235) and an **Ascot** teapot (£450-£550/$790-$1075).

Royal Winton Spring Glory: Tray from a bedside set (£50-£60/$90-$115).

Royal Winton Springtime: Preserve or honey pot with silver plated lid (£100-£120/$175-$235).

GRIMWADES (Royal Winton)

Tableware in Royal Winton Somerset Chintz. Total value £1500-£2000/$2625-$3915.

GRIMWADES (Royal Winton)

Royal Winton Stratford: A small rimmed soup or dessert dish (£180-£220/$315-$430) and a two–piece cruet set on a matching base (£250-£280/$440-$550).

Royal Winton Springtime: **Sexta** hot water lidded jug (£550-£650/$965-$1275).

Royal Winton Summertime: **Norman** shaped teapot (£300-£350/$525-$685).

Royal Winton 'Star Flower': Fruit dish in the **Humber** range (£70-£80/$125-$155).

Right: Royal Winton Summertime: Teapot in **Elite** shape (£450-£550/$790-$1075), jam pot in Chelsea shape (£160-£180/$280-$350).

GRIMWADES (Royal Winton)

Royal Winton and Crown Ducal Chintz. Centre charger and vases £200-£300/$350-$585; smaller pieces £50-£150/$90-$295.

GRIMWADES (Royal Winton)

Royal Winton **Summertime**: A wall clock (£150-£200/ $265-$390) and a small **Countess** teapot (£300-£350/ $525-$685).

Royal Winton **Sunshine**: A footed bon–bon dish (£220- £250/$385-$490); a stacking set of teapot, cream and sugar in the **Delamere** shape (£700-£800/$1225- $1565).

Royal Winton **Sunshine**: Bedside set (£900-£1000/ $1575-$1960).

Royal Winton **Sweet Nancy**: Two-handled oval sweetmeat dish (£75-£85/$130-$165).

Royal Winton Sweet Pea: Globe jugs (£400-£450/$700-$880; £375-£425/$655-$830; £280-£350/$490-$685).

Royal Winton Sweet Pea hors d'oeuvre dish (£300-£400/$525-$785); Marguerite coffee pot (£220-£250/$385-$490); Welbeck muffin dish (£280-£320/$490-$625); Old Cottage Chintz Bedside set (£800-£900/$1400-$1760); Marguerite Cream Jug (£60-£70/$105-$135).

GRIMWADES (Royal Winton)

Royal Winton *Sweet Pea:* A bedside set comprising a **Countess** teapot, a cup, a cream jug, an open sugar bowl and a toast rack (£1500-£1700/$2625-$3330), a biscuit barrel (£500-£600/$875-$1175), an **Athena** shape teapot (£750-£850/$1315-$1665), a 3-bar toast rack (£180-£220/$315-$430) and a pair of salad servers (£250-£300/$440-$585).

Royal Winton *Sweet Pea:* Bedside set (£1500-£1700/$2625-$3330).

Royal Winton *Sweet Pea:* Sugar shaker and spoon (£500-£600/$875-$1175) with Floral Feast **Ascot** jam pot and spoon (£250-£300/$440-$585).

Royal Winton Sweet Pea: Teapot in the Alban Shape (£700-£750/$1225-$1470).

Royal Winton Sweet Pea: Basket in the Essex shape 11"x6½"x5¼" high (£750-£850/$1315-$1665).

GRIMWADES (Royal Winton)

Royal Winton Sweet Pea: Athena hot water pot (£750-£850/$1315-$1665) and teapot (£750-£850/$1315-$1665).

Royal Winton Sweet Pea: Tea pot (£750-£850/$1315-$1665), coffee pot (£800-£900/$1400-$1760), condiment set (£200-£250/$440-$570), plate (£100-£120/$175-$235), jam pot (£180-£200/$315-$390) and jug (£750-£850/$1315-$1665).

Royal Winton Sweet Pea II: Shaped sandwich plate (£180-£200/$315-$390).

Royal Winton A selection of tea and coffee in **Royalty** (£750-£850/$1315-$1665), **Sweet Pea** (£750-£850/$1315-$1665), **Mayfair** (£600-£850/$1050-$1665), **Nantwich** (£700-£750/$1225-$1470) and **Kew** (£650-£750/$1140-$1470).

Royal Winton Tartans: An **Ascot** tea plate (£60-£70/$105-$135) and a 3-bar toast rack (£80-£100/$140-$195).

Royal Winton 'Tea Roses': Large triple tray in the **Rex** shape £140-£160/$245-$315.

GRIMWADES (Royal Winton)

Royal Winton **Triumph**: A large round bread and butter plate (£80-£90/$140-$175), a small cream jug in the **Globe** shape (£70-£80/$125-$155) and a small oval dish (£50-£60/$175-$115).

Royal Winton **Victorian**: Small tea plate in the **Ascot** shape (£40-£50/$70-$100).

Royal Winton Bedside sets.

GRIMWADES (Royal Winton)

Royal Winton Victorian Rose: An **Ascot** sandwich plate (£95-£115/$165-$225) and a 3-bar toast rack (£120-£150/$210-$295).

Royal Winton Victorian Rose: Platter and cake slice (£70-£85/$125-$165).

Royal Winton Violets: An oval sweetmeat dish with curving Art Deco style 'handles' (£120-£150/$210-$295).

Royal Winton Welbeck: **Hastings** milk and sugar (£250-£300/$440-$585) with **Perth** coffee pot (£1200-£1400/$2100-$2740).

Royal Winton Welbeck: An Art Deco shaped fruit bowl (£180-£220/$315-$430); a **King** shape cup and saucer (£100-£120/$175-$235).

Royal Winton Welbeck: **Gem** shape rose bowl (£450-£550/$790-$1075).

GRIMWADES (Royal Winton)

Various items in Royal Winton Chintz Ware, values range from £50-£300/$90-$585.

GRIMWADES (Royal Winton)

Royal Winton **Elite** teapot in Welbeck (£950-£1000/$1665-$1960).

Royal Winton Welbeck: **Ajax** shape teapot (4 cup size) (£800-£900/$1400-$1760).

Royal Winton Welbeck **Rosebud** basket shape, £600-£700/$1050-$1370, Sunshine **Rosebud** basket shape (£300-£400/$525-$785).

Royal Winton White Roses: A biscuit barrel in the **Rheims** shape (£300-£400/$525-$785).

Royal Winton Wild Flowers: An egg cup stand (minus the egg cups) (£50-£60/$90-$115) and a small butter pat dish in the **Trefoil** shape (£60-£70/$105-$135).

Royal Winton Winifred: Lidded **Candy** box, (£90-£100/$160-$195).

GRIMWADES (Royal Winton)

A range of modern chintz from Royal Winton.

GRIMWADES (Royal Winton)

Prototypes of the new Royal Winton limited edition figures commissioned from Royal Winton by Francis Joseph.

A special commission from Royal Winton by Francis Joseph – Florence, limited to 1000 pieces (RRP).

Another special commission from Francis Joseph – Royal Winton Welbeck – a beautiful historic piece limited to 1000

GRIMWADES (Royal Winton)   JAMES KENT

Royal Winton Welbeck, with alternative positioning of the plate.

James Kent **Apple Blossom** 2-pint teapot in Granville shape (£150-£200/$265-$390).

Left: James Kent **Apple Blossom** 9" plate, (£70-£80/ $125-$155).

Right: James Kent **Apple Blossom** octagon plate, (£75-£85/ $130-$165).

James Kent **Apple Blossom** Tennis set, (£65-£75/ $115-$145).

*James Kent **Autumn Flowers** tea plate (£50-£60/$90-$115).*

*James Kent **Crazy Paving**, shaped fruit bowl (£60-£80/$105-$155).*

*James Kent **Du Barry** teapot (£250-£300/$440-$585), egg cruet (£120-£150/$210-$295), plate (£30-£45/$55-$90).*

James Kent Du Barry butter dish (£125-£160/$175-$265).

A range of items in the Du Barry pattern.

JAMES KENT

*James Kent **Du Barry** fruit bowl (£70-£80/$125-$155).*

*James Kent **Florita** Coffee pot in the **Granville** shape (£650-£750/$875-$1050) together with Royal Winton **Summertime** teapot in the **Elite** shape (£600-£700/$655-$745).*

*James Kent **Florita** saucer to tennis set (£30-£40/$55-$80).*

*James Kent **Hydrangea (Black)** shaped dish 6½" (£75-£85/$130-$165).*

*James Kent **Hydrangea (White)** plate, (£35-£45/$60-$90).*

James Kent Lichfield (£60-£70/$105-$135).

JAMES KENT

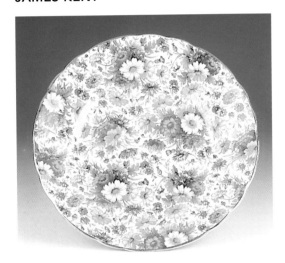

James Kent **Marigold** plate 7¾" diameter (£40-£50/$70-$100).

James Kent **Mille Fleurs** fluted nut dish in Chelsea shape (£55-£65/$95-$125).

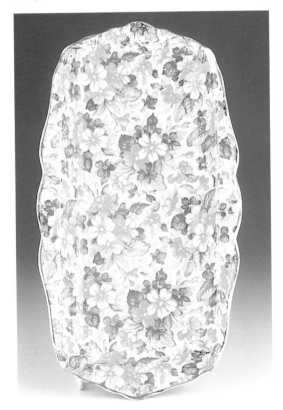

James Kent **Primula** sandwich plate in Jewel shape, 11" in length (£50-£60/$90-$115).

James Kent **Rosalynde** (£45-£50/$80-$100).

JAMES KENT

*James Kent **Rapture** cream and sugar set and sandwich plate (£65-£75/$115-$145). All in the Diamond shape.*

*James Kent **Rosalynde** 10" diameter cake plate (£70-£75/$125-$145).*

*James Kent **Roses** shaped dish (£50-£60/$90-$115).*

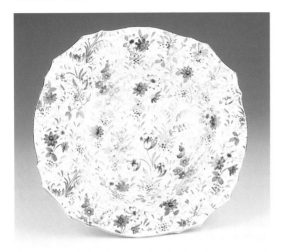

James Kent **Silverdale** sandwich plate (£40-£50/$70-$100).

James Kent **Tapestry** dessert plate 8½ diameter (£45-£55/$80-$110).

James Kent **18th Century Chintz** dessert plate 9¼" diameter (£55-£65/$95-$125).

Leighton Ware **Autumn Roses** cup and saucer (£40-£45/$70-$90).

W. R. Midwinter, **Brama** 10" plate (£40-£45/$70-$90).

W. R. Midwinter, **Coral** fruit bowl with plated rim (£80-£90/$140-$175).

Morley **Peruvian Lily** tea plate (£30-£40/$55-$80).

W. R. Midwinter, **Lichfield**, sugar sifter with chrome top (£70-£80/$125-$155).

Myott **Bermuda** square trinket dish (£50-£60/$90-$115).

Myott **Spring Flower**, oval candy dish 7¾" long (£75-£85/$130-$165).

Myott **Summer Flower**, sugar bowl (£40-£45/$70-$90).

PARAGON

Paragon **June Glory**, food warmer (£60-£70/$105-$135).

A G Richardson **Ascot** part of sponge dish (no base) (£30-£40/$55-$80).

A G Richardson **Canton**, shaped dish (£70-£80/$125-$155).

A G RICHARDSON (Crown Ducal)

A G Richardson **Blue Chintz**, pepper pot (£30-£40/$55-$80).

A G Richardson **Festival** plate (£40-£45/$70-$90).

A G RICHARDSON (Crown Ducal)

*A G Richardson **Florida** coffee saucer (no cup) (£15-£20/$26-$39).*

*A G Richardson **Grey Fruit** plate (£20-£35/$35-$70).*

*A G Richardson **Ivory Chintz**, biscuit barrel with silver plated handle and lid (£450-£550/$790-$1075).*

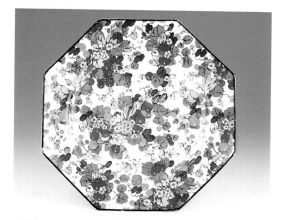

*A G Richardson **Ivory Fruit**, octagonal cake plate (£65-£75/$115-$145).*

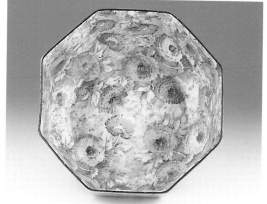

*A G Richardson **Marigold**, octagonal fruit bowl (£80-£100/$140-$195).*

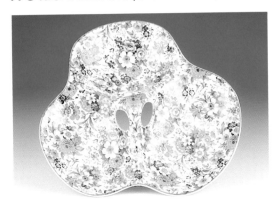

*A G Richardson **Mille Fleur**, three-lobed dish with cut-out handle (£80-£100/$140-$195).*

*A G Richardson **Peony**, oval dish 6" in length (£50-£60/$90-$115).*

*A G Richardson **Pink Chintz**, 10" diameter plate (£100-£120/$175-$235).*

*A G Richardson **Pink Chintz**, plate (£100-£120/$175-$235); vases (£350-£450/$615-$880); bowl (£250-£300/$440-$585).*

*A G Richardson **Primula** shaped oval dish, 9" in length (£80-£100/$140-$195).*

*Ridgways, (Bedford Works) **Autumn Flowers**, cake plate (£80-£100/$140-$195).*

RIDGWAYS

Ridgways, (Bedford Works) **Poppies**, *fruit bowl (£60-£80/$105-$155).*

J. Shaw (Burlington Ware) **Spring Daisies**, *tea plate (£35-£50/$60-$100).*

Ridgways, Potteries **Summer Flowers**, *3 tier cake stand (£65-£75/$115-$145).*

Shelley Green Daisy tea plate (£40-£45/$70-$90).

Shelley **Maytime**, *sugar bowl (£65-£75/$115-$145).*

*Shelley **Melody** sugar bowl (£50-£60/ $90-$115).*

*Shelley **Pink Summer Glory** (£40-£45/ $70-$90).*

*Shelley **Rock Garden** cup and saucer (£85-£95/$150-$185).*

*Shelley **Rock Garden**, tea plate (£40-£45/$70-$90).*

*Soho Pottery Ware **Sunningdale** octagonal tea plate (£35-£45/$60-$90).*

*Soho Pottery Ware **Tulips and Roses** octagonal tea plate (£40-£45/$70-$90).*

*John Tams Ware **Anemone** large tea plate (£40-£50/ $70-$100).*

*John Tams Ware **Blue Roses** tea plate (£30-£40/$55- $80).*

*Wade, **Butterfly Chintz** cream jug (£50-£60/$90-$115).*

*Wade, **Darwin** cake plates (£60-£70/$105-$135).*

*Wade, **Thistle** Chintz dish (£60-£70/ $105-$135).*

J. H. Weatherby (Falcon Ware), **Peruvian Lily** *(£50-£60/$90-$115).*

Wedgwood **Columbine** *cake plate (£70-£80/ $125-$155).*

Wedgwood **Cowslips** *sandwich tray (£60-£70/$105-$135).*

Wilkinson Mayflower teapot, £180-£225/$315-$440.

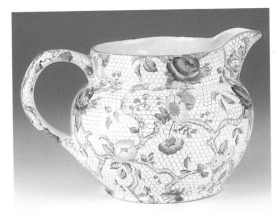

Arthur Wood, **Honeycomb Flowers** *large milk jug (£70-£80/$125-$155).*

Patterns and Price Guide

When referring to chintz ware, it is generally the tightly packed floral designs that is meant by the term. However, it can sometimes be difficult to draw a distinct line between chintz, sheet transfer patterns and all-over patterns. Therefore for ease of reference, all patterns, whether chintz, sheet transfer, or all-over design, have been included in the following list.

Another difficulty that faces the collector is the fact that some of the patterns are un-named. For ease of reference, these patterns have been given identifying names which can be seen written in quotes, such as 'Blue Tulip', 'Exotic Bird' and 'Rose Spray'.

An attempt has been made to describe and identify the flowers that make up the patterns, although botanical accuracy cannot be guaranteed as many of the flowers have been vaguely drawn and are unidentifiable. However, some are surprisingly accurately drawn and botanically correct, such as the *Eryngium Maritimum*, commonly known as *Sea Holly*, which can be seen on Fireglow (Black).

Dates and shapes are mentioned only if they can be verified. The information has been taken from various catalogues and advertising fly sheets, and from the pages of the *The Pottery Gazette*. No date is given unless it can established with an exact reference. Nevertheless, it is clear that the majority of the better chintz patterns were created and produced between the years 1932 and 1939.

The manufacturer's trademark stamped on the base of ware is a useful guide to dating. These marks were changed periodically and new ones introduced. However, some overlapping of dates occurs and precise dating cannot be guaranteed.

The prices of the following groups have been compiled by experts in the Chintz field both in the USA and UK. Because prices tend to go up and down, we have not been specific. Different markets exist for Chintz. You can buy at a trade show, or through a specialist, Internet or an auction house. It is simply not possible to be specific. Nor should we be. Generally the price of Chintz pottery is on the increase in any case. Our prices are a *guide* only. Buyers need to know the value of an item in broad terms. If you sell a piece to a dealer, he or she will have to sell on for a profit and therefore the price you achieve will be less than selling directly yourself.

We have divided the following into four groups. **Group A** is small individual items like Ashtrays (small); Bonbon dish; Bowls, (up to 7" diameter); Butter pat; Coaster; Demitasse; Nut dish; Plates, (up to 7" diameter); **Group B** is for larger items like Ashtray (large); Bowls (over 7" diameter); Egg cup, footed; Cake plate, tab/open handles; Plates (over 8" diameter); Salt and pepper sets; Teacup and saucer; Tennis set; Vase, bud; **Group C** part sets and unusual items such as Biscuit barrel; Butter dish; Cake plate, 8 square pedestal; Cake stand (2 tier/3 tier); Cake stand, chrome handle/base; Cake plate, with server; Canoe-shaped dish; Cheese keep; Compote, footed; Condiment set on tray; Cream and sugar on tray; Jam pot with liner; Jugs 5"-7"); Relish dish, small; Salt and pepper on tray; Sandwich trays; Salad bowl, chrome rim; Sauce boat and liner; Sugar shaker; Trivet; Toast rack (2 slice/4 slice); Vases; and **Group D** for full sets of items like Breakfast set; Coffee pot with cups; Hot water jug; Plate, 9"/10" octagonal; Teapot with cups; Teapot, stacking.

BARKER BROTHERS; (TUDOR WARE)

Established 1876, Meir Works, Barker Street, Longton, Staffordshire

Barker 1   Barker 2

'Blue Chintz (picture page 17)
Date of manufacture 1937+
Backstamp Barker 1
An all blue pattern, this shows sprays of leaves and blossom in white, highlighted with blue on a similar blue ground.

Group A	Group B	Group C	Group D
£30-£60	£100-£175	£200-£300	£350-£450
$55-$115	$175-$345	$350-$585	$615-$880

Butterflies (picture page 17)
Date of manufacture 1937+
Backstamp Barker 1
Brightly coloured butterflies in shades of rust, blue, yellow and pink intermingle with orchid- and chrysanthemum-like flowers in pink and white. Tiny dots of grey are formed in scroll patterns against the white ground.

Group A	Group B	Group C	Group D
£40-£80	£100-£200	£225-£300	£350-£450
$70-$155	$175-$390	$395-$585	$615-$880

'Hydrangeas' (picture page 17)
Date of manufacture 1937+
Backstamp Barker 1

Group A	Group B	Group C	Group D
£20-£40	£90-£150	£200-£275	£300-£375
$35-$80	$160-$295	$350-$540	$525-$735

Lorna Doone (picture page 17)
Date of manufacture unknown
Backstamp Barker 1
This pattern is difficult to date. A full page advertisement was inserted in *The Pottery Gazette* by A. J. Wilkinson in May 1949 which praised the new Lorna Doone design. The pattern was also produced by Midwinter under their Stylecraft backstamp which dates from 1961, although Midwinter probably did not use the pattern until after they took over Wilkinson's in 1964 (*see Midwinter*). The Midwinter pattern also appears to have later been called 'Bird Chintz', with some American collectors calling it 'Chickadee'.

Lorna Doone is an open pattern and depicts small birds in blue and yellow perched on the branches of what appear to be rose bushes. The flowers are picked out in shades of pink, yellow and blue. Tiny dots of blue and grey are arranged randomly, or in leaf shapes, to help obscure the white ground.

Group A	Group B	Group C	Group D
£40-£80	£120-£250	£300-£350	£400-£550
$70-$155	$210-$490	$525-$685	$700-$1075

'Peonies and Chrysanthemums' (picture page 17)
Date of manufacture 1937+
Pattern number 1212 – Backstamp Barker 2
A delicate pattern of combined flowers, such as peonies, shaggy chrysanthemums, briar roses and French marigolds, is shown in pink, white and yellow. Pale blue daisies and convolvulus and small green leaves, set against a white ground, give additional colour and interest.

Group A	Group B	Group C	Group D
£30-£50	£75-£150	£200-£300	£350-£450
$55-$100	$130-$295	$350-$585	$615-$880

'Trellis Roses' (picture page 18)
Date of manufacture 1930-1937
Backstamp BARKER BROS LTD ENGLAND set within two circles with a central fleur-de-lys
This vivid pattern shows pink and yellow roses on a trellis-like arrangement of budding branches. Clematis-like flowers in pink, cerise and blue are set against a background of deep yellow, merging with green.

Group A	Group B	Group C	Group D
£25-£40	£70-£150	£175-£250	£300-£400
$45-$80	$125-$295	$305-$490	$525-$785

BOOTHS LIMITED
Established 1891, formerly T. G. & F. Booth 1883-91, Church Bank Pottery, Tunstall, Staffordshire

Evesham (picture page 18)
Date of manufacture 1930s
Backstamp as illustration
Richly coloured fruits decorate the white ground, with additional tiny sprays of blossom in white, outlined in a dark brown. The fruit consists of purple grapes, pears shaded in yellow and dark pink, cherries in red, yellow and pale purple, and dark pink plums.

Group A	Group B	Group C	Group D
£35-£50	£70-£120	£150-£250	£300-£400
$60-$100	$125-$235	$265-$490	$525-$785

BRITISH ANCHOR POTTERY (REGENCY WARE)
Established 1884, Anchor Road, Longton, Staffordshire

'Apple Blossom' (picture page 18)
Date of manufacture 1950s
Backstamp 1952+ Regency in script with BRITISH ANCHOR ENGLAND EST 1884 below
and a crown above
This design features branching sprays of pink and white apple blossom and leaves on a thick cream ground. The pattern is enhanced by the addition of bright blue flowers and stylised green leaves.

Group A	Group B	Group C	Group D
£35-£60	£75-£150	£200-£300	£350-£450
$60-$115	$130-$295	$350-$585	$615-$880

BURGESS BROTHERS
1922-1939, Carlisle Works, Longton Staffordshire

'Daisies' (picture page 18)
Date of manufacture 1922-1939
Backstamp BURGESS WARE set within two circles surmounted by a crown
This light and spring-like pattern shows branching sprays of daisies in yellow, pink, white and rust. The sprays are widely spaced and the ground colour is white, but appears green due to the myriad of tiny 'squiggles' of colour.

Group A	Group B	Group C	Group D
£40-£65	£90-£150	£175-£275	£300-£400
$70-$125	$160-$295	$300-$540	$525-$785

CHAPMANS LONGTON LTD (ROYAL STANDARD)
Established 1916, Albert Works, Longton, Staffordshire

Virginia Stock (picture page 18)
Date of manufacture 1940s
Backstamp as illustration
The flower is attractively depicted in natural colours of light and dark pink, lilac and white. There are additional touches of yellow and the leaves are green. The ground colour is white.

Group A	Group B	Group C	Group D
£35-£60	£80-£160	£190-£300	£350-£450
$60-$115	$140-$315	$335-$585	$615-$880

ELIJAH COTTON (LORD NELSON WARE)

Established 1880, Nelson Pottery (from 1889), Hanley, Staffordshire

The two backstamps are sometimes found overprinted on one another. The pattern name is sometimes included, either printed in the circle or can be found written in script elsewhere

Anemone (picture page 18)
Date of manufacture 1930s
Pattern number 2446
Backstamp as illustration
Anemone was an open stock pattern and was also used by John Tams (Tams Ware) and by John Shaw & Sons (Burlington Ware). When used by Elijah Cotton, it can be found with the pattern number 2446. Vividly coloured anemonies, accompanied by green leaves, are set on a white ground. The flowers are picked out in blue, pink and yellow.

Group A	Group B	Group C	Group D
£25-£40	£45-£60	£95-£150	£250-£400
$45-$80	$80-$115	$165-$295	$440-$785

Black Beauty (picture page 19)
Date of manufacture 1930s
Backstamp as illustration
This is one of the more desirable Lord Nelson pattern. Black Beauty has yellow and pink tea roses set on a black ground. Sprays of lilac, and foliage in various shades of green, enhance the pattern.

Group A	Group B	Group C	Group D
£35-£55	£65-£85	£100-£220	£450-£600
$60-$110	$115-$165	$175-$430	$790-$1175

Briar Rose (picture page 19)
Date of manufacture 1930s
Backstamp as illustration
The flower is depicted in various shades of rich pink and has a green centre. Smaller flowers in yellow are also shown, as are small half-hidden buds in blue. The foliage is minimal, and the ground colour is formed by a splattering of grey and pale green, giving an overall green effect.

Group A	Group B	Group C	Group D
£30-£45	£45-£75	£90-£140	£300-£400
$70-$90	$80-$145	$160-$275	$525-$785

Country Lane
Date of manufacture c1930s
Backstamp as illustration
Small meadow flowers in cerise and blue are set on a white ground. Larger, unidentifiable flowers in yellow and rust are accompanied by dark green leaves.

Group A	Group B	Group C	Group D
£20-£25	£30-£40	£45-£100	£225-£350
$35-$50	$55-$80	$80-$195	$395-$685

Green Tulip (picture page 19)
Date of manufacture 1930s
Backstamp as illustrated
Sprays of spring flowers and dark green foliage make up this delightful pattern. White narcissi are teamed with yellow primulas and small flowers of a gentian blue, while similar sprays, with tulips instead of narcissi, dominate in a bold cerise colour. The whole is set on a pretty green ground which is broken up by white polka dots.

Group A	Group B	Group C	Group D
£35-£55	£65-£75	£75-£200	£425-£475
$60-$110	$115-$145	$135-$390	$745-$930

Heather (picture page 19)
Date of manufacture 1930s
Pattern number 2750
Backstamp as illustration
Delicate sprays of heather are set against a white ground which is covered in ochre dots, making it appear a pale creamy yellow shade. The heather bells are in pink, yellow, white, and a dark shaded blue. The foliage is green and a blue-green.

Group A	Group B	Group C	Group D
£25-£40	£45-£55	£60-£150	£300-£325
$45-$80	$80-$110	$105-$295	$525-$635

Marigold
See also James Kent Mille Fleurs picture page 62
Date of manufacture 1930s – Pattern number 2122
Backstamp as illustration
Used by Elijah Cotton with the pattern number 2122 this was another open stock pattern. It can also be seen on ware made by A. G. Richardson (Crown Ducal) and James Kent, who called it Mille Fleurs.

The pattern shows a variety of summer flowers in various shades of yellow, pink and blue, all with green leaves and set on a white ground. The flowers consist mainly of French marigolds, narcissi, campanula (bell flowers) and flat-petalled roses.

Group A	Group B	Group C	Group D
£20-£40	£45-£55	£50-£150	£275-£325
$35-$80	$80-$110	$90-$295	$480-$635

Marina (picture page 19)
Date of manufacture 1930s
Registered number 821468
Backstamp as illustration
Branched sprays of roses, mainly in a cerise pink with the occasional yellow bloom, are set against a white ground, given depth by grey leaves. Other flowers are painted in shades of yellow, orange, blue and pink, and add extra colour.

Group A	Group B	Group C	Group D
£25-£35	£40-£50	£60-£125	£300-£350
$45-$70	$70-$100	$105-$245	$525-$685

Pansy (picture page 19)
Date of manufacture c1930s
Pattern number 2207
Backstamp as illustrated
An open stock pattern, Pansy was also issued by Royal Albert and Shelley. It is an extremely striking pattern with the flower shown in a vivid indigo/violet. Tiny heart shaped leaves are done in a soft green and the whole set against a creamy white ground.

Group A	Group B	Group C	Group D
£25-£45	£55-£65	£60-£150	£275-£450
$45-$90	$95-$125	$105-$295	$480-$880

Rosetime (picture page 20)
Date of manufacture 1930s
Registered number 829287
Backstamp Pattern name in script with CHINTZ below followed by REG No. 829287
Bouquets of cabbage roses in pink, yellow and white are spread widely across this pattern. Tiny bunches of smaller, unidentifiable, flowers in pink and yellow are also seen, with the background composed of tiny blue leaves against a white ground.

Group A	Group B	Group C	Group D
£30-£40	£50-£65	£60-£150	£350-£450
$55-$80	$90-$125	$105-$295	$615-$880

Royal Brocade (picture page 20)
Date of manufacture 1930s
Backstamp as illustration
Flowers and leaves in a very pale yellow, highlighted with grey, are set against a rich burgundy ground. The flowers are enlivened by small blue centres.

Group A	Group B	Group C	Group D
£25-£30	£40-£65	£45-£100	£250-£300
$45-$60	$70-$125	$80-$195	$440-$585

Skylark (picture page 21)
Date of manufacture c1950s
Backstamp as illustrated but with a facsimile of Nelson's column in the centre Flat-petalled flowers and buds in white, yellow and blue are accompanied by leaves in white, and blue outlined with black. The same striking blue is used for the ground colour.

Group A	Group B	Group C	Group D
£25-£40	£45-£60	£60-£120	£240-£300
$45-$80	$80-$115	$105-$235	$420-$585

DEANS (1910) LIMITED

In existence 1910-1919, Newport Pottery, Burslem, Staffordshire

Deans 1

Deans 2

Delton Ware (picture page 21)
Date of manufacture 1910-1919
Backstamp Deans 2
The pattern consists of mauve and deep pink branching chrysanthemums. Small daisy-like flowers are grey, outlined in black, and set against a black ground.

Group A	Group B	Group C	Group D
£25-£40	£55-£70	£80-£150	£350-£450
$45-$80	$95-$135	$140-$295	$615-$880

Lucerne Ware (picture page 21)
Date of manufacture 1910-1919
Pattern name Chintz
Backstamp as Deans 1 but with Lucerne Ware in script and not Delton Ware
Random whirls of black outlines against dark grey, form the background, while large, pale pink flowers lighten the pattern, together with smaller yellow blooms and white daisies. A pheasant-like bird with a yellow body and brown wings can also be seen.

Group A	Group B	Group C	Group D
£25-£40	£55-£70	£80-£150	£350-£350
$45-$80	$95-$135	$140-$295	$615-$685

EMPIRE PORCELAIN COMPANY LTD

Established 1896, Empire Works, Stoke, Staffordshire

Empire 1

Empire 2
The numbers 2B52
suggest a date mark

Empire 3

Empire 4
with date mark

'Black Marguerite' (picture page 21)
Date of manufacture 1940s – Registered number 15683
Backstamp 1940s-1950s Empire 1
Although the flowers in this pattern are in colours of blue (pale and darker), pink and yellow, with green leaves, the predominant colour is that of blue against a black ground. Various meadow or wild flowers can be identified, such as speedwell, marsh marigold, flax, cranebill and what is possibly a wild peony.

Group A	Group B	Group C	Group D
£25-£35	£40-£45	£50-£60	£150-£175
$45-$70	$70-$90	$90-$115	$265-$345

Golden Wattle (picture page 21)
Date of manufacture 1950s – Registered number 15683
Backstamp Empire 1, Empire 2
The wattle flower is, perhaps, better known in the UK as mimosa, and that is what the pattern represents. Sprays of the blossom in bright yellow, together with its distinctive green leaves, are set against patches of blue which partly obscure the ivory ground.

Group A	Group B	Group C	Group D
£25-£30	£30-£35	£45-£55	£150-£200
$45-$60	$55-$70	$80-$110	$265-$390

Lilac Time (picture page 21)
Date of manufacture 1930s – Registered number 15683
Backstamp 1930s Empire 3
Lilacs, primroses and forget-me-nots are delicately portrayed in pastel colours of cerise, lilac, yellow and blue. The ground colour is a pale green, softened by the addition of tiny florets outlines in white. The pattern was also produced in a cream or ivory ground, however this colourway is less common.

Group A	Group B	Group C	Group D
£30-£50	£50-£60	£65-£75	£275-£350
$55-$100	$90-$115	$115-$145	$480-$685

Rosalie (picture page 22)
Date of manufacture 1930s
Backstamp Empire 3 with date mark G–36
Stylised garden flowers and leaves are arranged in sprays across a white ground broken up by fine geometric lines in pale brown. The flowers are in colours of bright orange, yellow, pink and blue; the leaves are green.

Group A	Group B	Group C	Group D
£30-£50	£60-£70	£100-£150	£300-£400
$55-$100	$105-$135	$175-$295	$525-$785

Water Lily (picture page 22)
Date of manufacture 1930s – Registered number 15683
Backstamp Empire 3
A host of water lilies and buds in colours of blue, yellow and pink, supported by dark green leaves, float on water described by dashes of blue and yellow; small reed-like leaves are also in the water.

Group A	Group B	Group C	Group D
£25-£35	£35-£40	£45-£60	£150-£175
$45-$70	$60-$80	$80-$115	$265-$345

T.G. GREEN & CO.
Established 1864, Church Gresley, Nr Burton-on-Trent, Derbyshire

Harmony (picture page 22)
Date of manufacture c1930s
An open stack pattern that was used by several companies, including James Kent, Hollinshead & Kirkham, and A.G. Richardson (Crown Ducal).

Tea Roses are shown in shades of pale orange, peach and yellow, with narcissi in white. Other unidentifiable flowers are in blue and pale orange. Pale green leaves accompany the bouquets of flowers and the ground colour is white.

Group A	Group B	Group C	Group D
£25-£40	£50-£75	£100-£175	£300-£400
$45-$80	$90-$145	$175-$345	$525-$785

GRIMWADE (ROYAL WINTON)
Established 1885, Winton Pottery, Stoke-on-Trent, Staffordshire
It was thought that the prefix Royal was added to the Winton trade name in the 1930s. However, research has shown that Royal Winton ware was being made in 1896. The name was used again in 1917/18 (See Backstamp 2). It then disappeared, being revived in about 1929, when Grimwades introduced their new Royal Winton Ivory. However, examples of Marguerite chintz, made in 1928, show the Royal Winton backstamp used in the familiar Art Deco style. It is interesting to note that the Home Office have no record of the company contacting them regarding the prefix.

In 1945, as a result of World War II, potteries were divided into six groups and obliged to mark their wares with a letter or letters of the alphabet, according to which group they belonged. They were also restricted to making tea and dinner ware, cooking ware including pie dishes, washstand sets, chamber pots, hot water bottles and stoppers and rolling pins.

The 1948 Year Book, issued by *The Pottery Gazette* shows that Grimwades were designated category 'A'. The letter had to be stamped indelibly under the glaze and the ruling was in force for some years after the war. For an example, see Backstamp 8. This would indicate that ware showing the 'A' as part of the backstamp was made after the war years.

Backstamp 1

Grimwades backstamp c1906+. Also found without the words WINTON WARE. The mark shows the globe which is sometimes found surmounted by a crown and accompanied by the letters GB for Grimwade Brothers c1885+.

Backstamp 2

c1917-19+.

Backstamp 3

c1922+. The letters S.P. stand for Semi-Porcelain.

Backstamp 4

Art Deco style mark c1928+ found on items including Marguerite chintz. This mark was previously thought to date from the mid-1930s.

Backstamp 5

Art deco style mark c1934+. Note the semi-circular MADE IN ENGLAND mark also present. This can sometimes be found alone, transfer printed in either green and black, and with no other Royal Winton backstamp.

Backstamp 6

Art Deco style mark c1937+. This backstamp seems to have been used only on Quilt and Tartans. Note the registration numbers for Canada which appear to be a date.

Backstamp 7

Summertime COPYRIGHT Wright Tyndale & van Roden Inc ENGLAND. Blue transfer printed copyright mark in script and capitals, found only on some Summertime pieces.

Backstamp 8

Royal Winton MADE IN ENGLAND A. The script mark c1951+. Note the 'A' mark used from 1945. The illustration also shows the registration numbers for Canada, Australia, New Zealand and the USA transfer printed in gold.

Backstamp 9

The fine script mark transfer printed in black c1964+. This was the backstamp used by Royal Winton after the takeover by Howards.

Backstamp 10

This is a mystery back-stamp, possibly used by the Staffordshire Potteries after they took over Royal Winton in 1979.

Backstamp 11

Grimwades backstamp found on a Marguerite cup and saucer. The word Grimwades spans the globe carried by Atlas. This mark was used from 1910 onwards until it was replaced by a stylised mark similar to Backstamp 4 c1934-39

Backstamp 12

JAPAN. The word is transfer printed in red with no other identifying backstamp. This implies that Japanese copies were made and imported into the UK, and that the pattern is not by Royal Winton.

Anemone c1930s (picture page 22)
Pattern number 4801, 4809
Backstamp 4 with the words 'Hand Painted' in script, transfer printed in dark blue, a greeny blue, and mid-blue.
The flowers in this design represent the spring flowering anemone, also known as the Windflower and which is related to the Wood Anemone.
  This is a transfer-printed pattern with a hand painted infill on the flowers. It can be found

in two colourways. The first has hand-painted creamy anemones which have pale to deep orange centres. These are set against well defined green leaves and are accompanied by pale lavender Michaelmas daisies, with small flower heads enamelled in turquoise blue. The ground colour is a dark almost navy blue.

The second colourway has vivid yellow hand-painted anemones with red enamelled centres. The Michaelmas daisies are a muted pink, and are set against pale green leaves on a mid-blue ground. There is no enamelling on the small flower heads apart from a spot of red in the centres.

Group A	Group B	Group C	Group D
£20-£35	£35-£50	£50-£150	£250-£375
$35-$70	$60-$100	$90-$295	$440-$735

Balmoral c1950s (picture page 23)
Pattern number 374
Backstamp 4, 8
Densely packed flowers and leaves are shown against a black ground. Some of the flowers are unidentifiable, but there are pink roses, shaded pink anemones, pale pink irises, white daisies with yellow centres, several meadow flowers, sprays of blue flower heads, and sprays of orange and yellow budding flower heads.

The name refers to the castle in Scotland.

Group A	Group B	Group C	Group D
£45-£60	£60-£75	£150-£200	£450-£575
$80-$115	$105-$145	$265-$390	$790-$1125

Beauvais c1917 (picture page 22)
Pattern number 4221
Backstamp 1. Sometimes found printed in addition to Backstamp 3
Large pink flowers predominate, and are set against a black ground, with leaves portrayed in soft shades of green and tan. Small flowers in bright orange can also be seen. The cock bird is perched on a branch and is coloured in blue with pink wing feathers and brown tail feathers. The breast feathers are in yellow and tan while his crest is orange. The hen bird is painted in muted shades of yellow, pink, blue and brown.

A Grimwade's catalogue for 1917, shows the Beauvais pattern was used on vases in the Tiber, Rydal, Tulip and Pisa shape, with covered vases being made in the Chinese and Ovoid shape. Jardinieres (which could have an accompanying pedestal) were made in the shapes of Greek, Delphic and Argyle, while a washstand set in the Wem shape is also illustrated.

Group A	Group B	Group C	Group D
£20-£35	£50-£75	£135-£225	£450-£500
$35-$70	$90-$145	$235-$440	$790-$980

Bedale c1930s (picture page 22)
Pattern number 1703, 4969
Backstamp 4
This is an alternative colourway to Summertime, the second pattern issued by Royal Winton. The roses on Bedale are yellow instead of pink, and the smaller briar roses are shown as pink and not yellow. However, the white daisies and bluebells remain the same in both patterns.

The name refers to a town in Yorkshire.

Group A	Group B	Group C	Group D
£35-£50	£50-£65	£150-£200	£375-£550
$60-$100	$90-$110	$265-$390	$655-$1075

Beeston c1930s (picture page 22)
Pattern number 2203
Backstamp 4
A dramatic rendering of pink and yellow roses accompanied by green leaves set against a black ground. The quality of transfer printing is extremely high and pieces have an attractive glossy finish. The pattern was used on angular Art Deco shapes as well as those of a more traditional nature.

The name refers to towns in Cheshire, Norfolk, Bedfordshire, Nottingham and West Yorkshire.

Group A	Group B	Group C	Group D
£45-£75	£75-£120	£220-£300	£450-£600
$80-$145	$130-$235	$385-$585	$790-$1175

'Birds and Tulips' c1930s (picture page 24)
Pattern number 1084
Backstamp GRIMWADES ROYAL WINTON IVORY ENGLAND transfer printed in green.
A very stylised Art Deco pattern showing birds printed in pink, red and blue perched on branches amongst sprays of pink and yellow tulips, bunches of yellow and red seeds and grey and green leaves. The other flowers in red, pink, yellow and dark blue are extremely stylised and botanically unrecognisable. The white ground is stippled with blue dots.

Group A	Group B	Group C	Group D
£25-£35	£60-£85	£175-£250	£500-£600
$45-$70	$105-$165	$305-$490	$875-$1175

'Blackberries' c1930s (picture page 24)
Backstamp 4
The pattern shows autumnal branches of a fruit-bearing blackberry bush. The colours are very realistic and are set against a white ground.

Group A	Group B	Group C	Group D
£40-£50	£80-£100	£200-£250	£700-£800
$70-$100	$140-$195	$350-$490	$1225-$1565

'Black Daisies' c1951 (picture page 24)
Backstamp 8
A sheet pattern design of flowers outlined in black, accompanied by black leaves and set against a spherical arrangement of black dots. All on a vivid yellow ground.

Group A	Group B	Group C	Group D
£40-£60	£90-£110	£220-£260	£700-£800
$70-$115	$160-$215	$385-$510	$1225-$1565

'Blocked Roses' c1930s (picture page 24)
Pattern number 3329
Backstamp 4
A dramatic background of striped geometric shapes arranged in a 'blocked' pattern gives impact to the rather simple pattern of tea roses. A central bouquet is picked out in shades of pink with light green foliage. Smaller flowers are enamelled in blue, and printed yellow flowers have additional blue enamelling.

Group A	Group B	Group C	Group D
£50-£60	£85-£110	£230-£270	£750-£850
$90-$115	$150-$215	$405-$530	$1315-$1665

Blue Anemone – see **Chintz**

'Blue Jade' (picture page 24)
Pattern number 4594
Backstamp 4
The name refers to the sprays of turquoise blue flowers which appear to be a dwarf variety of the delphinium known as Blue Jade. The other blossoms in the pattern are possibly briar or rambling roses and are in shades of pink and blue. A few leaves are additionally hand-painted in gold. The background colour is a smudgy blue on white. It can also be found in different colourways – pink or yellow and orange, for example. The pattern is known to some collectors as 'Ice Flowers'.

Group A	Group B	Group C	Group D
£30-£40	£80-£125	£250-£300	£400-£500
$55-$80	$140-$245	$440-$585	$700-$980

'Blue Tulip' (picture page 25)
Pattern number 1178
Backstamp GRIMWADES ROYAL WINTON IVORY ENGLAND transfer printed in green.
Deep blue tulips with paler shading and outlined in yellow are set against yellow leaves. Smaller flowers are also in yellow, accentuated by grey leaves and occasional branches of deep blue leaves. The ground colour is black.

Group A	Group B	Group C	Group D
£20-£35	£30-£50	£60-£100	£200-£325
$35-$70	$55-$100	$105-$195	$350-$635

Carnation c1930s (picture page 25)
Backstamp 4
This was mentioned in the American press in 1933 and was referred to as a chintz pattern, despite the overall effect being that of a sheet pattern. The bold design consists of shaded pink carnations, highlighted with vivid orange/red hand enamelling. The pointed leaves are white, while green oval shapes are decorated with grey stripes interspersed with black and white. The ground colour is a deep blue. Examples without the red enamelling were also produced and these have an altogether lighter appearance.

Group A	Group B	Group C	Group D
£30-£35	£35-£40	£60-£85	£150-£200
$55-$70	$60-$80	$105-$165	$265-$390

Cheadle c1950s (picture pages 25 and 26)
Pattern number 311
Backstamp 4, 8
Registration numbers for Canada 1951 and USA 166273.
Summer flowers defy recognition in this pattern. There are, what appear to be, white and yellow briar roses set against green rose leaves, with additional blue harebells, and small yellow and cerise flower heads. These are all set against a creamy white ground.
   The name refers to towns in Staffordshire and Greater Manchester in Lancashire.

Group A	Group B	Group C	Group D
£40-£60	£75-£125	£175-£250	£450-£625
$70-$115	$130-$245	$305-$490	$790-$1225

Chelsea c1950s (picture page 26)
Pattern number 455
Backstamp 4
Registration numbers for Canada 1952.
A striking pattern predominantly featuring large pink roses and white briar roses with blue centres. These are accompanied by sprays of orange flowers, pale blue buds and green leaves, set against a black ground. The pattern is easily confused with Esther on smaller pieces.
   Name refers to an area in London.

Group A	Group B	Group C	Group D
£45-£80	£90-£125	£150-£250	£450-£750
$80-$155	$160-$245	$265-$295	$790-$1470

Chintz c1930s (picture page 26)
Pattern number 2836
Backstamp 4
The flowers in this pattern are autumn flowering anemones. The blooms are in shades of red and blue and there are splashes of green leaves. The remaining foliage is blue and there is no ground colour to be seen.

Group A	Group B	Group C	Group D
£20-£35	£30-£40	£80-£150	£200-£325
$35-$70	$55-$80	$140-$295	$350-$635

Clevedon 1934 (picture page 26)
Pattern number 1844
Backstamp 4
Branching sprays of pink and yellow roses accompanied by green leaves dominate this pattern, with smaller daisy-like flowers in yellow, white and blue giving added colour. The background is cream, stippled with tiny yellow dots, giving the appearance of a pale yellow ground. There is a deep pink or cerise edging to the ware. On some examples of Clevedon, the white flowers are replaced by those of a deep blue.
   Clevedon offers an alternative colourway to the Cranstone pattern. The colours of the flowers are the same, except that the white flowers on Clevedon are blue in Cranstone and the stippling is of a vivid green.
   The pattern was recommended to the trade by *The Pottery Gazette* in January 1934.
   Name refers to a town at the mouth of the Severn near Bristol, Avon.

Group A	Group B	Group C	Group D
£35-£75	£75-£85	£220-£275	£650-£775
$60-$145	$135-$165	$385-$530	$1140-$1515

Clyde c1930s-1940s (picture page 26)
Pattern number 5637 (brown) 5315 (green)
Backstamp 4
This pattern was made in two colourways, both on a white ground. Pale apricot and yellow primroses are dotted singly, accompanied by green leaves. Alternatively, the flowers are pink and yellow set against brown leaves.
   Name refers to the river and area near Glasgow in Scotland.

Group A	Group B	Group C	Group D
£20-£35	£30-£40	£60-£100	£200-£275
$35-$70	$55-$80	$105-$195	$350-$540

Cobwebs c1930s (picture page 27)
Backstamp 4
This rarely seen pattern shows small scattered flowers in pink and yellow, together with green leaves, set against a background of dark blue lines arranged in a spider's web design.

Group A	Group B	Group C	Group D
£20-£40	£90-£130	£190-£230	£300-£400
$35-$80	$160-$255	$335-$450	$525-$785

Cotswold c1950s (picture page 27)
Pattern number 408
Backstamp 8, 9
Registration numbers for Canada 1952 and Australia 29774.
Apple blossom buds and harebells trim a central bouquet of unidentified flowers in pink, yellow and blue. A spray of pink roses is matched with smaller flowers in a pale rust. The ground colour is a very clear white.
Name refers to a range of English hills.

Group A	Group B	Group C	Group D
£15-£60	£50-£60	£175-£200	£500-£650
$26-$115	$90-$115	$305-$390	$875-$1275

Cranstone 1934 (picture page 27)
Pattern number 1154, 2256
Backstamp 4
Branching sprays of pink roses accompanied by green leaves dominate this pattern, with blue and yellow daisy-like flowers giving added colour. The ground colour is white, accentuated by vivid green dots.

Cranstone is an alternative colourway to Clevedon. The flowers are of identical colouring but the stippled background dots are green in Cranstone, yellow in Clevedon.

Again, like Clevedon, this pattern was recommended to the trade by the *The Pottery Gazette* in January 1934, when it was mis-spelled as Cranston. It was again mentioned, this time correctly spelled, in April 1935, in a report on the exhibition at Olympia. 'Good business was done with the new relief-modelled tablewares, and the 'Pelham' and 'Cranstone' chintz patterns were also very well received – more particularly so, perhaps, because the Queen (Queen Mary) purchased both of these patterns.'

Origin of name unknown

Group A	Group B	Group C	Group D
£45-£75	£75-£95	£250-£275	£680-£800
$80-$145	$130-$185	$440-$540	$1190-$1565

Crocus (Black) – see Triumph

Crocus (White) 1939 (picture page 27)
Pattern number 111
Backstamp 8
Bunches of yellow and blue crocuses, accompanied by sprays of pink and blue flowers, are set against a white ground. The pattern is identical to Black Crocus (above) apart from the ground colour. Items in Crocus were exhibited at Olympia in 1939 and the Royal Winton stand was visited by Queen Mary, the Duke of Kent and the Princess Royal. The Royal party bought many pieces of ware including Crocus.

Group A	Group B	Group C	Group D
£35-£65	£65-£75	£230-£275	£500-£600
$60-$125	$115-$145	$405-$540	$875-$1175

Cromer c1930s (picture page 28)
Pattern number 2078
Backstamp 4
Registration numbers for Australia 15540
A slightly more unusual pattern with widely spaced bouquets of pink roses and yellow, pink and blue flower heads, small daffodils and pendulous pink blooms (Dicentra) set against a barred black ground.
 The name refers to a town in Norfolk.

Group A	Group B	Group C	Group D
£20-£35	£30-£45	£90-£115	£280-£325
$35-$70	$55-$90	$160-$225	$490-$635

Delphinium Chintz 1931 (picture page 28)
Pattern number 9889.
Backstamp GRIMWADES ROYAL WINTON IVORY
The Delphinium flower was first used in 1930 on Savoy shaped table ware made in Royal Winton Ivory, where sprays of the flower were widely set against a cream/white ground. The pattern was also used on toilet ware of the Savoy shape.
 It appeared as a densely packed chintz pattern in 1931 and it is likely that it was the third chintz pattern issued by Grimwades. The full page advertisement in *The Pottery Gazette* in September 1932 details it as, 'An attractive Royal Winton adaptation of a popular Summer Flower'.
 Although it featured in advertising before Summertime, it is clear from the written copy in *The Pottery Gazette* that Summertime was the second pattern issued.
 According to the advertisement, articles supplied were tea and coffee sets, sandwich and fruit sets, cheeses, cake plates, egg sets, cruet sets, salad bowls, marmalade jars, sugars and creams, sweet dishes, footed sweets (also known as bon bon dishes), celery trays, jugs (all sizes and various shapes), teapots (all sizes and various shapes), and teapot stands.
 The arching sprays of delphiniums are seen in cerise, mid-blue and dark blue and are accompanied by green leaves. The ground colour is white.
 Shapes made in this pattern include a Duval jug, a Globe jug, a Fife sandwich tray, an octagonal tea plate, a footed sweet dish, a King cup and saucer and a Countess tea pot.

Group A	Group B	Group C	Group D
£20-£45	£45-£50	£50-£135	£150-£450
$35-$90	$80-$100	$90-$265	$265-$880

Dorset 1940s, 1950s, (picture page 28)
Pattern number 274 (pink), 294 (brown)
Backstamp 9
This is a sheet transfer pattern showing yellow petunias, shading from pale to darker hues, with pink centres and set against a white ground almost hidden by swirling pink flowers and tiny pink leaves.
 Name refers to a county in Southern England.

Group A	Group B	Group C	Group D
£20-£35	£30-£50	£40-£100	£100-£300
$35-$70	$55-$100	$70-$195	$175-$585

Eleanor c1950s (picture page 28)
Pattern number 375
Backstamp 8
The light and pretty design consists of a sprigged pattern of roses, together with various accompanying flowers in pink, yellow, blue and white. The gaps between the sprigs of flowers are interspersed with tiny stylised flower heads. The ground colour is white.

Group A	Group B	Group C	Group D
£20-£35	£60-£90	£150-£275	£350-£475
$35-$70	$105-$175	$265-$540	$615-$930

English Rose c1950s (picture page 29)
Pattern number 381
Backstamp 8
Registration number Canada 1951
One of the more delicate chintz patterns. The pale pink roses are accompanied by even paler blue flowers, with green and yellow leaves set against a creamy yellow ground.
   At first glance, this pattern might be confused with that of June Roses, but close examination will reveal the differences between the two. In addition, English Rose has gilding on the rim, whereas the edging of June Roses is silvered.

Group A	Group B	Group C	Group D
£45-£85	£80-£120	£150-£300	£350-£850
$80-$165	$140-$235	$265-$585	$615-$1665

Estelle c1950s (picture page 29)
Pattern number 423
Backstamp 8
Registration number Canada 1952; Australia 29775
Sprays of flat pink, yellow and pale lavender flowers are accompanied by apple blossom buds and green leaves set against a cream ground. The pattern is light and airy.

Group A	Group B	Group C	Group D
£30-£45	£50-£65	£125-£225	£350-£550
$55-$90	$90-$125	$220-$440	$615-$1075

Esther c1950s (picture page 29)
Pattern number 473
Backstamp 4
Registration number Canada 1952
A dramatic and vivid pattern. Deep pink roses, Crane's Bill (Geranium) flowers, yellow daisies and buttercups and small blue flower heads are seen against a glossy black ground. It can easily be confused with Chelsea on smaller pieces.

Group A	Group B	Group C	Group D
£40-£50	£70-£110	£175-£325	£595-£800
$70-$100	$125-$215	$305-$635	$1040-$1565

Evesham c1950s (picture page 30)
Pattern number 404
Backstamp 8
Registration number Canada 1951; Australia 29099; New Zealand 6484; USA 166274
An aptly named pattern, referring as it does to the rich and bountiful orchards of the Vale of Evesham situated in Gloucestershire and Worcestershire.

The pattern depicts various groups of fruit: apples, pears oranges, plums, cherries, grapes, strawberries, pomegranates and figs, all set against a cream ground. The effect is one of warm autumn colours and is very pleasing.

Group A	Group B	Group C	Group D
£60-£95	£100-£200	£300-£425	£500-£1200
$105-$185	$175-$390	$525-$830	$875-$2350

'Exotic Bird' c1930s (picture page 30)
Pattern number 301262
Backstamp GRIMWADES ROYAL WINTON IVORY transfer printed in green.
Brightly coloured pheasant-like birds perch on flowering branches. The birds are in colours of yellow, turquoise and warm red. The chrysanthemum-style flowers are in the same colours with leaves in turquoise and pale brown. The ground colour is cream.

Group A	Group B	Group C	Group D
£25-£45	£65-£90	£100-£150	£300-£450
$45-$90	$115-$175	$175-$295	$525-$880

Fernese 1925 (picture page 30)
Pattern number 8786
Backstamp 4
This sheet transfer printed design was advertised by Grimwades in 1925 and was originally called Fernese Diaper ware, having a triangular motif edging the wares. The ferns and butterflies were shown in white against a blue ground and the edging was in black and gold. Later Fernese ware can be seen without the diaper border and with the butterflies coloured in shades of yellow, pink and blue, apricot, with a large butterfly having red, turquoise and yellow wings. The ground colour has deepened to a mid-blue.

Group A	Group B	Group C	Group D
£25-£30	£40-£50	£60-£80	£100-£200
$45-$60	$70-$100	$105-$155	$175-$390

Fibre Roses c1919 (picture page 31)
Pattern number 3458
Backstamp 1
The pattern is set on a wide band against a rather indeterminate but busy pattern of tiny fern-like leaves in a beige colour. The pattern on the band consists of pink roses with green leaves alternating with sprays of lilac, all set on a black ground. The pattern within the band was used extensively by Grimwades on various backgrounds; the fern-like ground was named Fibre.

Group A	Group B	Group C	Group D
£25-£40	£60-£100	£150-£225	£300-£400
$45-$80	$105-$195	$265-$440	$525-$785

Fireglow (Black) c1950s (picture page 31)
Pattern number 533 – Backstamp 8
This is a pattern of dramatic orange pod-like flowers (identified as Montbretia) combined with a blue flower with holly-like leaves (Eryngium Maritimum – common name Sea Holly). In addition, starry white flowers with green leaves curling in tendrils are set against a black ground.

It is totally unlike the white Fireglow pattern listed below. However, several pieces of both patterns – all bearing backstamps with the pattern name of 'Fireglow' – have confirmed the existence of two Fireglow patterns, each one entirely different to the other.

Group A	Group B	Group C	Group D
£25-£40	£50-£70	£90-£175	£325-£400
$45-$80	$90-$135	$160-$345	$570-$785

Fireglow (White) c1930s (picture page 31)
Pattern number 2510 – Backstamp 4
In complete contrast to the Fireglow (Black) above, this pattern has a very spring-like air to it. It features bunches of pink roses and flat yellow flowers, together with sprays of daffodils, blue bell-like flowers (possibly Scilla) and pink pendulous flowers (Dicentra). These bouquets are set against a white background outlined with grey pebbles or bubbles.

Group A	Group B	Group C	Group D
£30-£50	£60-£90	£125-£175	£350-£475
$55-$100	$105-$175	$220-$345	$615-$930

Floral Feast c1930s (picture page 31)
Pattern number 1394 – Backstamp 4
Widely spaced bunches of primula-like flowers feature in a rich blue, pale pink, yellow and orange. There are additional twiggy sprays of blossom, small daisies and green leaves all set against a creamy ground. Despite the brightness of individual colouring, the whole presents a rather pale and delicate appearance.

Group A	Group B	Group C	Group D
£30-£50	£90-£165	£200-£350	£400-£475
$55-$100	$160-$325	$350-$685	$700-$930

Floral Garden (picture page 32)
Pattern number 4547, 4546 – Backstamp 4
The drooping, pendulous flower used in this pattern has been identified as Jacobinia pauciflora, sometimes also known as Justicia, and can be seen in three colourways. Items having a white ground have the Jacobinia in pink, shading to yellow at the tips. The pattern also includes large yellow roses, pink tulip-like blossoms, pink bell flowers, yellow and pink convolvulus and several starry flowers in white, outlined with purple and yellow. The leaves are green and the background is composed of grey leaves.

In the blue ground colourway, the Jacobinia flower is pale yellow, the roses are pale lavender and the chrysanthemum-like flower is in shades of pink. The background leaves are entirely blue.   Floral Garden is also available in a green colourway. The roses are shaded yellow and pink, the convolvulus is blue, with the Jacobinia flower in pink shading to cream. The leaves are tan against a background of mid-green leaves.

Group A	Group B	Group C	Group D
£20-£35	£40-£75	£95-£155	£175-£300
$35-$70	$70-$145	$165-$305	$305-$585

Florence c1950s (picture page 32)
Pattern number 472
Backstamp 4, 8
Registration numbers for Canada 1953
The vivid pink of carnations draws the eye to this pattern. Also featured are cream carnations and Amaryllis belladonna flowers (sometimes known as the Belladonna Lily) in a creamy yellow, plus a myriad of small blue and pink flowers which almost conceal the black ground. The colours are vivid and the transfer printing is excellent.

Group A	Group B	Group C	Group D
£55-£90	£115-£175	£300-£400	£900-£1100
$95-$175	$200-$345	$525-$785	$1575-$2155

Florette 1930 (picture page 32)
Pattern number 9594
This was advertised in a Grimwades catalogue for 1930 and is a sheet transfer pattern rather than a tight chintz. The stylised roses can be seen in pink and yellow with a 'halo' of mid-blue. The leaves are a reddish brown and are set against a white ground.

According to the Grimwades catalogue, the ware was made in the following shapes: Greek coffee pot, Duval jug (3 sizes), Octron sweet, Globe jug (4 sizes), Rex cheese dish (3 sizes), Elite and Countess teapots, Dane bowl, Lotus honey jar, Stafford fruit, Crown bowl, Fife sandwich tray, 5" octagonal plate, King tea cup and saucer, and an Imperial coffee cup and saucer.

Group A	Group B	Group C	Group D
£45-£70	£95-£175	£225-£375	£600-£700
$80-$135	$165-$345	$395-$735	$1050-$1370

'Gold Leaves' c1930s (picture page 32)
Pattern number 4501 (cream) 4586 (green)
Backstamp 8 (in gold)
A highly gilded all-over pattern of tiny gold leaves interspersed with small flat flower heads enamelled in turquoise and yellow. Ground colours were of either cream or green.

Group A	Group B	Group C	Group D
£20-£35	£50-£90	£150-£250	£350-£450
$35-$70	$90-$175	$265-$490	$615-$880

'Grapes and Roses' c1902 (picture page 33)
Pattern number 4203
Backstamp 1
Sprays of flowers in pink, blue, purple, white and yellow, together with clusters of grapes, cover the surface of the piece. Green leaves give additional interest while tiny green irregular circles give texture to the white ground. A frieze of pink and white roses is set on a wide black horizontal band against vertical stripes of white and beige.

Group A	Group B	Group C	Group D
£20-£35	£50-£90	£100-£200	£300-£4000
$35-$70	$90-$175	$175-$390	$525-$7840

Hampton Chintz c1913 (picture page 33)
Pattern number 544, 561, 562, 564, 579 (varying colourways). Pattern number 596 illustrated
Backstamp: Crown with the words ROYAL HAMPTON WARE (COPYRIGHT) GRIMWADES
An open pattern of roses in shades of pink and yellow can be seen, randomly placed on a white ground. Other flowers are in yellow, blue and pink, with small sprays of convolvulus shown in blue. The pattern was used on Octagon shaped dinner ware and was also produced in the Newlands shape which had round plates. It was also used in wide bands on toilet ware.

Group A	Group B	Group C	Group D
£30-£50	£70-£110	£125-£225	£300-£400
$55-$100	$125-$215	$220-$440	$525-$785

Hazel c1930s (picture page 33)
Pattern number 2208
Backstamp 4
The clear crisp colours of this pattern are enhanced by the mottled black ground. A large bouquet of flowers, consisting of pink and yellow roses, yellow daffodils and white narcissi, is edged by lilac tulips and purple wisteria. The pattern is interspersed with delicate green leaves. The same pattern, on different ground colours, features in both Spring and Welbeck but, in Hazel, the tulips are less well defined and the wisteria almost indistinguishable, so giving roses priority as a motif.

Group A	Group B	Group C	Group D
£45-£70	£80-£125	£225-£300	£675-£800
$80-$135	$140-$245	$395-$585	$1180-$1565

Jacobean c1913 (picture page 33)
Pattern number 3000
Backstamp 1
The pattern, a copy of an early 17th century tapestry, shows large white vine leaves, shaded with pale grey, and accompanied by cerise grapes, set against a black ground. This striking pattern is faintly lustred, which adds to its appeal. The new pattern was an instant success with royalty when George V and Queen Mary visited the Potteries in 1913, and the Queen was delighted to receive a gift of a Mecca Foot Warmer in the Jacobean pattern.

Group A	Group B	Group C	Group D
£25-£45	£60-£115	£175-£300	£500-£600
$45-$90	$105-$225	$305-$585	$875-$1175

Jacobina – see **Floral Garden**

Joyce-Lynn c1950s (picture page 33)
Pattern number 275
Backstamp 8
Cerise anemones and bright blue convolvulus, together with yellow daisies having ragged petals, are set against a lush background of green leaves. There is no ground colour visible.

Group A	Group B	Group C	Group D
£30-£75	£65-£75	£150-£200	£550-£625
$55-$145	$115-$145	$265-$390	$965-$1225

Julia c1930s (picture pages 34 and 35)
Pattern number 109
Backstamp 4, 8
The apparently green background to this pattern is formed from tiny white flowers outlined in green. The flowers that feature predominantly are cerise, yellow and pale pink tea roses decorated with green leaves. There are additional sprays of small blue flower heads and deep pink briar roses.

Group A	Group B	Group C	Group D
£65-£95	£100-£160	£300-£375	£1000-£1250
$115-$185	$175-$315	$525-$735	$1750-$2445

June Festival c1950s (picture page 35)
Pattern number 139 (navy)
Backstamp 8 (plain version) and Backstamp 9 (coloured version).
This pattern appears identical to May Festival but is transfer printed in a different colourway. The ground colour illustrated is wine or maroon and the white pansy flowers are shaded in the same colour. The example showing coloured flowers would appear to be hand painted. The flowers are shaded in colours of yellow, blue and lavender, enhanced by green leaves.

Group A	Group B	Group C	Group D
£20-£35	£40-£55	£100-£200	£350-£450
$35-$70	$70-$110	$175-$390	$615-$880

June Roses c1930s (picture page 36)
Pattern number 1924, 1945 (silver trim), 2036 (green trim)
Backstamp 4. Also found with only the words MADE IN with the word ENGLAND curved below, transfer printed in green (see Backstamp 5).
It can be quite easy to confuse this pattern with that of English Rose, although, when compared side by side, the two are quite easily distinguishable from each other. The colour in June Roses is a touch more definite and, in addition to the sprays of pink roses, June Roses also has sprays of unopened rosebuds and sprigs of wisteria. Both backgrounds are of a creamy yellow colour. The rim decoration on June Roses is silvered.

Group A	Group B	Group C	Group D
£45-£85	£100-£145	£225-£300	£600-£850
$80-$165	$175-$285	$395-$585	$1050-$1665

Kew c1950s (picture pages 36 and 50)
Pattern number 240
Backstamp 4, 8
A rather confusing mixture of summer flowers combine to create a very pretty pattern. Pink roses nudge pink, yellow and blue daisies, and overlook pink and deep blue cornflowers. There are also some rather strange-looking dahlia-like flowers which have alternating petals of orange and white. All are set on a cream ground.

There is also possibly a blue colourway of Kew; the flowers are the same colours as above, but the ground colour is pale blue. There could be several reasons for this. It could be that the unglazed biscuit was blue rather than white, or maybe the transfer printing process became discoloured in the kiln; it may even have been a trial piece. It is possible that the mystery will never be solved as no other blue pieces have yet been reported.

The name refers to an area in London.

Group A	Group B	Group C	Group D
£25-£60	£55-£75	£190-£225	£500-£625
$45-$115	$95-$145	$335-$440	$875-$1225

Kinver 1934 (picture page 36)
Pattern number 2254
Backstamp 4
The pattern consists basically of two sprays or bouquets of flowers. One features roses in pink and a deep improbable blue, yellow tulips with cerise tips, pink chrysanthemums and dark blue convolvulus. The other spray also has pink roses and dark blue convolvulus plus pink daisies, bright blue flower heads and a large pink daffodil with a yellow trumpet. All these flourish against a stippled yellow ground. Kinver was recommended to trade buyers by *The Pottery Gazette* in January 1934. The name refers to a town near Stourbridge.

Group A	Group B	Group C	Group D
£45-£75	£75-£125	£275-£325	£700-£800
$80-$145	$130-$245	$480-$635	$1225-$1565

Majestic c1930s (picture page 36)
Pattern number 3311
Backstamp 4
A striking pattern of pale cerise anemones and vivid blue carnations, accompanied by green and ochre leaves and set against a black ground. This is an alternative colourway of the pattern Royalty which appeared in 1936. The flowers in Royalty are deeper in colour and are set against a pale yellow ground.

Group A	Group B	Group C	Group D
£45-£85	£80-£120	£220-£300	£950-£1100
$80-$165	$140-$235	$385-$585	$1665-$2155

Marguerite 1928 (picture pages 36)
Pattern number 9467 (blue trim), 9432 (gold trim)
Backstamp 4, 11
Registration numbers for Canada 1951
The first time this name was used by Grimwades for a pattern was in 1892 when the company was still trading as Grimwade Bros. The pattern was described as having widely spaced flowers picked out in red and pale blue, and finished with gold 'clouds'.

However, the chintz pattern Marguerite, with its pattern of white daisies, yellow and cerise flowers and sprays of bluebells set against a beige ground, made its appearance in 1928. It was used in two ways on toilet ware of the Octron shape. Pattern number 9609 had wide panels of Marguerite chintz alternating with sections of plain colour and the toilet sets were available in colours of blue, pink or old gold. Pattern number 9467 was also used on toilet sets which were available in an all-over chintz design with the rim of the ware edged in dark blue. Leonard Grimwade's youngest daughter, Janet, was told that the design was taken from a cushion cover being embroidered by her mother.

The new chintz design – the forerunner of so many – was to prove an instant success for the company and was subsequently used on table ware. *The Pottery Gazette* maintained, in their issue for November 1929, that 'the theme [of the design] is reminiscent of the charm of the countryside, the shapes being new and unquestioningly appealing'. They also recommended the ware as being 'eminently suitable for the Christmas trade'.

Early shapes in Marguerite include Elite teapots, Duval and Globe jugs, Greek coffee pots, King tea cups, Hurstmere sugar bowls, Winton cream jugs, Vera cream jugs, Stafford fruit bowls and long trays, Rex cheese dishes, large Crown bowls, and Orleans sandwich trays and plates. Some Marguerite tableware was also made by Atlas China while under the Grimwades' ownership.

Group A	Group B	Group C	Group D
£25-£45	£40-£50	£125-£175	£370-£450
$45-$90	$70-$100	$220-$345	$650-$880

Marion c1950s (picture page 37)
Pattern number 324
Backstamp 8
Registration numbers for Canada 1951
A delicate pattern in pastel colours. The flowers appear to be white Amaryllis belladonna (sometimes known as the Belladonna lily) with yellow throats, pink carnations and unidentifiable daisy-like flowers in shades of pink, blue and yellow. These are set against a white ground decorated with green circles of irregular outline.

Group A	Group B	Group C	Group D
£45-£80	£75-£100	£200-£250	£600-£750
$80-$155	$130-$195	$350-$490	$1050-$1470

Mayfair c1950s (picture pages 37 and 50)
Pattern number 392
Backstamp 8
Registration numbers for Canada 1951.
A rather widely spaced pattern having bouquets of chrysanthemums in cerise and pale rust and flat, blue anemone-like flowers, a few small cerise buds and trailing green leaves. The pattern is crisply depicted and the ground colour is an unusual pale greeny-yellow.
   The name refers to an area in London.

Group A	Group B	Group C	Group D
£35-£60	£60-£95	£225-£300	£650-£750
$60-$115	$105-$185	$395-$585	$1140-$1470

May Festival c1950s (picture page 37)
Pattern number 135 (navy), 139 (black)
Backstamp 9
At first sight this pattern could be mistaken for June Festival. The flowers and leaves are identical, but the colourway is slightly different. May Festival has a dark blue ground with the peony flowers and leaves in white, tinged here and there with pale to mid-blue. It can also be found on a black ground, and sometimes with hand painting on the flowers, similar to June Festival.

Group A	Group B	Group C	Group D
£20-£50	£45-£50	£110-£135	£350-£475
$35-$100	$80-$100	$195-$265	$615-$930

Merton c1920s (picture pages 38)
Backstamp as 1 but without the words Winton Ware
An exotically-coloured pheasant-like bird is portrayed centrally, perched on a branch. Vivid pink roses, together with amber and purple chrysanthemums and green foliage surround the bird. A butterfly in shades of ochre, rust and blue can be seen below the main bird, with smaller birds also included in the pattern. All is set against a vivid blue ground.

Group A	Group B	Group C	Group D
£30-£50	£40-£60	£100-£125	£300-£400
$55-$100	$70-$115	$175-$245	$525-$785

Morning Glory c1950s (picture page 38)
Backstamp 9
A very bold pattern of the convolvulus flower can be seen twining its way across the sheet transfer printed pattern. Both flowers and leaves are in white with pale pink detailing. The ground colour is a deep wine, almost maroon colour with an alternative colourway of a jet black ground.

Group A	Group B	Group C	Group D
£20-£50	£45-£50	£105-£135	£385-£475
$35-$100	$80-$100	$185-$265	$675-$930

Nantwich c1950s (picture pages 38 and 50)
Pattern number 291
Backstamp 4
This features bunches of pink roses, some with yellow tones to the petals. The carnations are also in the same pink, again some having yellow toned petals. Large yellow daisy-like flowers are interspersed with small blue speedwells and the ground colour is black.
    The name refers to a town near Crewe in Cheshire.

Group A	Group B	Group C	Group D
£35-£65	£60-£90	£150-£225	£500-£650
$60-$125	$105-$175	$265-$440	$875-$1275

Old Cottage Chinz c1930s (picture page 38)
Pattern number 9632
Backstamp 4
Cerise pink roses are enhanced by small flat blue flowers and green and yellow leaves. The other flower shown, accompanied by green leaves, closely resembles Allium, being of a globular shape formed by a myriad of tiny pink star shaped florets. The background is formed of tiny grey circular outlines on a white ground.

Group A	Group B	Group C	Group D
£30-£50	£50-£75	£100-£160	£360-£425
$55-$100	$90-$145	$175-$315	$630-$830

Orient c1950s (picture page 39)
Pattern number 471 – Registration numbers for Canada 1953
Backstamp 8
A striking design which is more of a sheet transfer pattern rather than chintz. A white and green water lily floats on a black ground which is broken up by tiny yellow wavelets. The pattern is enhanced by sprays of pink blossom, possibly Prunus (Cherry) with green leaves. Green and yellow butterflies separate the flower clusters.

Group A	Group B	Group C	Group D
£20-£35	£35-£55	£90-£125	£250-£350
$35-$70	$60-$110	$160-$245	$440-$685

Oriental Fantasy c1950s (picture page 39)
Backstamp 9
A lively scene featuring oriental fishermen set against a black background. The men can be seen fishing and carrying their catch from moored boats to the harbour jetty. Other boats are dotted about and the scene also includes an island volcano surrounded by cherry trees. Blue waves enliven the picture, while grey and orange clouds seem to foretell a storm.
  Scattered cherry blossoms and leaves can also be seen.

Group A	Group B	Group C	Group D
£40-£50	£80-£120	£200-£300	£400-£500
$70-$100	$140-$235	$350-$585	$700-$980

'Paisley' 1923 (picture page 39)
Pattern number 8152
Backstamp 4
A busy all-over pattern, the paisley design can also be seen on items by manufacturers other than Royal Winton. Grimwades issued it in colourways of green and rust. The colours are vivid in the green colourway, with additional hues of turquoise, orange and yellow. The paisley swirls are accompanied by stylised flowers and leaves and are set against a white ground. The rust colourway uses shades varying from pale apricot through pale orange to deep rust. There is some minimal additional decoration in yellow. The ground colour is white.
  There is also a blue colourway where colours of deep blue, tan and green are seen on a white ground, but this seems to appear mainly on ware by other manufacturers.
  The design was illustrated in a Grimwades catalogue for 1923 when it was shown in an Elite shape jug.

Group A	Group B	Group C	Group D
£20-£35	£25-£45	£60-£90	£250-£325
$35-$70	$45-$90	$105-$175	$440-$635

Pebbles c1930s (picture page 39)
Pattern number 1727
Backstamp 4
A sheet transfer printed pattern of simple style, Pebbles can be found in two colourways of green or a pale creamy yellow. The pattern consists of irregular pebble shapes, outlined in brown. The green alternates from a pale to a slightly darker hue. Pieces do not seem to bear the pattern name and this was identified by a Royal Winton employee.

Group A	Group B	Group C	Group D
£25-£50	£90-£130	£220-£300	£300-£400
$45-$100	$160-$255	$385-$585	$525-$785

Pekin (picture page 40)
Pattern number 320
Backstamp 9. Also found with; GRIMWADES ROYAL WINTON IVORY ENGLAND, and J-W. Co. STAFFORDSHIRE ENGLAND ROYAL WINTON (Backstamp 10). Some pieces are marked Hand Painted.
Registration number Canada 1951
This willow-pattern design was made with four different ground colours. The black colourway has subtle shadings of yellow, ochre and tan, with the highlights on the pagoda, bridge and boat picked out in a raspberry pink. Accompanying flowers and leaves are in shades of pink, white and yellow.

The pattern on the cream colourway is a little more well defined. Pink is used, as in the black version, but the trees and the foreground to the pagoda are picked out in delicate shades of green.

The blue colourway is again similar to the black Pekin but like the cream version, uses shades of green for the trees. The foreground of the pagoda is in shades of yellow and green.

The red colourway is quite striking and is possibly the first version to have been introduced, having the ROYAL WINTON IVORY backstamp. The pagoda roof, bridge and boat are in blue, the trees in green and lilac, while the foreground is green. There is additional hand enamelling which adds to the richness of the colouring.

Group A	Group B	Group C	Group D
£25-£45	£50-£75	£120-£200	£280-£375
$45-$90	$90-$145	$210-$390	$490-$735

Pelham 1935 (picture page 39)
Pattern number 2201
Backstamp 4
This would appear to be the first in the range of needlepoint or sampler designs. Pelham shows a pretty design of pink, blue and yellow flowers set in an ornamental urn of pale blue having darker blue crossing lines. Small bouquets of flowers intersperse the urns and the background is composed of a graph paper design on a white ground. On close examination, Pelham can be seen to be a reduced version of the Sampler pattern.

The pattern was mentioned in *The Pottery Gazette* in April 1935 when reporting on the exhibition at Olympia. 'Good business was done with the new relief-modelled tablewares, and the 'Pelham' and 'Cranstone' chintz patterns were also very well received – more particularly so, perhaps, seeing that the Queen (Queen Mary) purchased both of these patterns.'

Group A	Group B	Group C	Group D
£20-£40	£40-£50	£120-£145	£300-£350
$35-$80	$70-$100	$210-$285	$525-$685

Peony c1950s (picture page 40)
Backstamp 9
This is a very similar design to both June and May Festival, but having the flowers differently arranged. The ground colour is black and the peony flowers are shown in shades of white and grey.

Group A	Group B	Group C	Group D
£20-£45	£40-£65	£90-£135	£350-£425
$35-$90	$70-$125	$160-$265	$615-$830

Queen Anne 1936 (picture page 40)
Pattern number 2995
Backstamp 4, 8
Registration number Canada (impressed) 1951; Australia 15541
This is another of the needlepoint or sampler patterns issued by Royal Winton, the first of which appears to be Pelham. The pattern consists of bouquets of flowers in pink, blue and yellow, accompanied by green leaves and executed in a cross-stitch style. The background is of grey graph paper on an ivory ground.

The Pottery Gazette previewing the British Industries Fair, commented in February 1936, 'Several fresh patterns in old English chintzes will also be on view, including a very pleasing 'sampler' design which has been named Queen Anne.'

Queen Mary, too, must have approved of the pattern, as an invoice from Grimwades, dated 15th July 1936, shows that Her Majesty ordered a Bowl No 1 in the Fife shape at a cost of 2/6d (12½ pence).

Group A	Group B	Group C	Group D
£20-£40	£40-£55	£90-£145	£200-£350
$35-$80	$70-$110	$160-$285	$350-$685

Queen Mary Chintz c1910 (picture page 40)
Pattern number 595 (plain ground), 4459 (illustrated)
Backstamp Atlas China
Registration number (GB) 472879
This delicate pattern shows pink and yellow roses, together with small Campion-like flowers and blue Convolvulus, set on a white ground. This is additionally decorated with tiny blue dots and sprigs of flowers and leaves in the same colour. Extra ornamentation is added by gilding to the rim of the pieces.

Group A	Group B	Group C	Group D
£20-£40	£50-£60	£90-£150	£200-£300
$35-$80	$90-$115	$160-$295	$350-$585

Quilt c1938 (picture page 40)
Pattern number 4515
Backstamp 6
Registration number (GB) 824107 (c1938); Canada 10.1.38 (which appears to be a date); Australia 17469
Quilt is a pattern which lives up to its name, and consists of various sections representing a patchwork of floral fabrics. They are arranged haphazardly and are in colours of pink, blue and black, with touches of yellow here and there. There is no ground colour to be seen.

Group A	Group B	Group C	Group D
£20-£35	£30-£40	£50-£100	£200-£325
$35-$70	$55-$80	$90-$195	$350-$635

Richmond 1938 (picture page 41)
Pattern number 4229
Backstamp 4
The pattern on Richmond consists of an abundant design of bright yellow daffodils and white narcissi, with sprays of green leaves, bluebells and pink and blue hyacinths set against a pale green ground. The name refers to towns in North Yorkshire and Greater London.

Group A	Group B	Group C	Group D
£45-£85	£75-£110	£150-£275	£600-£850
$80-$165	$130-$215	$265-$540	$1050-$1665

Ripon c1917 (picture page 41)
Pattern number 4211 (yellow ground), 4218 (pale turquoise ground)
Backstamp 1 but with Grimwades above and Winton on the strap across the Globe
Large pink tea roses are randomly placed on leafy branches. Small flowers in purple and yellow add extra colour. The ground colour is pale turquoise blue; when the pattern was used on a yellow ground, all the flowers are pink

Group A	Group B	Group C	Group D
£30-£50	£60-£120	£175-£300	£600-£700
$55-$100	$105-$235	$305-$585	$1050-$1370

'Rosebuds' c1922 (picture page 41)
Pattern number 4461
Backstamp 3
Small, budding roses, together with short stems and small green leaves, are picked out in yellow, pink and blue against a black ground. This pattern was used extensively for tableware and also for toilet sets. It is possible that this pattern is Royal Dorset, but this cannot be proved conclusively at present.

Group A	Group B	Group C	Group D
£30-£40	£50-£70	£100-£200	£500-£600
$55-$80	$90-$135	$175-$390	$875-$1175

Rose du Barry (picture page 41)
Backstamp 4
The pattern is one that has been used by several manufacturers other than Royal Winton. However, the piece illustrated is marked with Backstamp 4. The design has a delicate appearance and consists of pale pink roses and violets accompanied by curving leaves in green and pale purple. The white ground enhances the pastel colours. The pattern has also been seen marked with the pattern name Chelsea Rose and issued by James Kent.

Group A	Group B	Group C	Group D
£25-£40	£45-£65	£100-£175	£300-£425
$45-$80	$80-$125	$175-$345	$525-$830

'Rose Spray' c1950s (picture page 41)
Backstamp 9
A light and airy design of pink roses, smaller blue flowers and orange and yellow daffodils, all widely set against a white ground.

Group A	Group B	Group C	Group D
£20-£40	£50-£70	£90-£150	£300-£400
$35-$80	$90-$135	$160-$295	$525-$785

'Rose Sprig' c1940s (picture page 41)
Backstamp 4
This is a widely spaced pattern showing sprigs of flowers comprising a pink rose, a yellow starry flower, and several small violets, set against a vivid yellow ground.

In April 1940, *The Pottery Gazette* reported: 'Among other new styles there is a series of treatments with underglaze blown backgrounds relieved by scattered sprays of chintz. There are three different backgrounds – pink, green and yellow.The series has only been on the market a few weeks, but we learn that it has already secured good business.' Close examination of 'Rose Sprig' would indicate that is possibly to this pattern that *The Pottery Gazette* was referring.

Group A	Group B	Group C	Group D
£30-£50	£70-£150	£200-£325	£400-£450
$55-$100	$125-$295	$350-$635	$700-$880

'Roses' c1922 (picture page 42)
Pattern number 4325
Backstamp as 3 but without the words Winton Ware
Half-opened tea roses in shades of yellow and deep pink are accompanied by leaves of green, shading to a deep pink. The black ground is enlivened by a profusion of daisy-like flowers painted in turquoise blue and green. Large purple leaves give additional colour. The effect is extremely striking. The pattern is quite large and appears to be limited to toilet sets.

Group A	Group B	Group C	Group D
£30-£50	£70-£150	£200-£325	£400-£450
$55-$100	$125-$295	$350-$635	$700-$880

Rose Violet – see Rose du Barry

Royal Hampton Ware – see Hampton Chintz

Royalty 1937 (picture pages 42 and 50)
Pattern number 3079
Backstamp 4, 8
This consists of a striking pattern of pale cerise anemones and vivid blue carnations accompanied by green and ochre leaves set against a pale yellow ground. Royalty is an alternative colourway to Majestic which features flowers in the same colour but on a black ground.

An invoice sent by Grimwades to Queen Mary on the 20th February 1937 shows that she ordered a Stafford twin tray, a covered muffin, a Chrysta powder box and a Burke powder box in the Royalty pattern. It is interesting to note that the twin tray cost 1/3d, the covered muffin cost 1/6d, while the powder boxes cost 10d each. In post-decimal money (new pence), that is respectively 6¼p, 7½p, 4p.

Group A	Group B	Group C	Group D
£55-£90	£125-£175	£200-£375	£725-£950
$95-$175	$220-$345	$350-$735	$1270-$1860

Rutland 1933/34 (picture page 42)
Pattern number 1470
Backstamp: words ROYAL WINTON (curved) with WINTON (below) transfer printed in green (see Backstamp 5). Also GRIMWADES ROYAL WINTON IVORY ENGLAND transfer printed in green.
Registered number (GB) 768965
A showy pattern of white, pink, ochre and blue daisies arranged in a bouquet, with smaller daisies in rust and blue, and accompanied by sprays of what appears to be yellow lilac. The ground colour is white. Name refers to an English county.

Group A	Group B	Group C	Group D
£30-£55	£60-£75	£125-£215	£400-£525
$55-$110	$115-$145	$220-$420	$700-$1030

Sampler (picture page 42)
Identical to Pelham, but printed as an enlarged version, Sampler is a pretty design of pink, blue and yellow flowers set in an ornamental urn of pale blue having darker blue crossing lines. Small bouquets of flowers intersperse the urns and the background is composed of a graph paper design on a white ground.

Group A	Group B	Group C	Group D
£20-£40	£60-£125	£150-£225	£300-£400
$35-$80	$105-$245	$265-$440	$525-$785

Shrewsbury c1950s (picture page 43)
Pattern number 418
Backstamp 8
Registration numbers for Canada 1952; Australia 29776.
Although the pattern consists of daisies, like Rutland, this has been given a far more serene treatment. The flowers are mainly of a soft pink, some petals tinged with yellow, with the occasional white daisy. The leaves are almost fern-like, the ground colour a creamy yellow/white.
Name refers to a town in Shropshire

Group A	Group B	Group C	Group D
£40-£60	£60-£100	£125-£200	£450-£625
$70-$115	$105-$195	$220-$390	$790-$1225

Silverdale – see **James Kent Silverdale**

Somerset c1930s (picture page 43)
Pattern number 1420 (gold trim), 1611 (blue trim)
Backstamp 4
The flower featured appears to closely resemble the lilac but, as the leaves are those of a delphinium, one can safely assume that it is the delphinium which is portrayed. Sprays of the blossom are closely packed together and are in colours of pink, blue and yellow, giving an effect totally unlike that of the Delphinium Chintz pattern, where the sprays are slightly more widely set. There is an accompaniment of green leaves, and the ground colour is a creamy yellow.
Name refers to a county in Southern England.

Group A	Group B	Group C	Group D
£45-£85	£80-£120	£175-£300	£600-£900
$80-$165	$140-$235	$305-$585	$1050-$1760

Spring c1930s (picture page 43)
Pattern number 2506
Backstamp 4
This shows a large bouquet of flowers consisting of pink and yellow roses, yellow daffodils and white narcissi. Pale lilac tulips and purple wisteria edge the bouquet which is interspersed with delicate green leaves. The same pattern features in both Hazel and Welbeck but against differently coloured backgrounds. The ground colour on Spring is white irregularly partitioned by small pebble shapes in grey.

Group A	Group B	Group C	Group D
£45-£75	£80-£175	£225-£325	£650-£800
$80-$145	$140-$345	$395-$635	$1140-$1565

Spring Glory c1950s (picture page 43)
Pattern number 401, 402
Backstamp 9
A riotous display of yellow cowslips and pink, blue and white wild wood anemones forms this pattern. The green leaves are those of the cowslip and the black ground emphasises the delicate pastel colours.

Group A	Group B	Group C	Group D
£20-£40	£50-£80	£100-£200	£300-£425
$35-$80	$90-$155	$175-$390	$525-$830

Springtime 1932 (picture pages 43 and 45)
Pattern number 10017
Backstamp MADE IN with ENGLAND curved below, transfer printed in green (see
Backstamp 5)
A vigorous treatment of tulips features a bunch of the flowers in a bold cerise colour, shading to yellow at the base of each tulip. The tulips are accompanied by flat yellow and blue flowers and foliage set on a white ground.

The pattern was advertised in *The Pottery Gazette* in April 1932 when it was declared that the pattern was much in demand.

Group A	Group B	Group C	Group D
£30-£50	£55-£85	£125-£200	£400-£575
$55-$100	$95-$165	$220-$390	$700-$1125

'Star Flower' c1930 (picture page 45)
Pattern number 178 (pink), 281 (brown)
Backstamp 4 in gilt
This is a very pretty pattern when done in the pink colourway, the brown colourway being less attractive. An arrangement of roses, peonies and daisies is handpainted in pastel colours of yellow, pink, blue and mauve, the leaves being a delicate green. Tiny star-shaped flowers are picked out in white against the ground colour.

Group A	Group B	Group C	Group D
£20-£40	£50-£75	£100-£200	£300-£400
$35-$80	$90-$145	$175-$390	$525-$785

Stratford c1950s (picture page 45)
Pattern number 493
Backstamp 8
Registration number Canada 1953
Cerise and yellow tulips accompanied by green leaves decorate this attractive pattern. The flowers are complemented by small sprays of lilac plus their leaves, although, at first sight, the lilac can be mistaken for bunches of blackberries. The ground colour is in subtle shades of a delicate blue.

Name refers to an area in London.

Group A	Group B	Group C	Group D
£65-£100	£125-£250	£350-£500	£900-£1300
$115-$195	$220-$490	$615-$980	$1575-$2545

Summertime 1930/31 (picture pages 45 and 47)
Pattern number 775 (gold trim), 1612 (green trim)
Backstamp 4, 7, 8. Also seen marked with the words MADE IN ENGLAND in black transfer
printed capitals. Some items were marked with the words Summertime COPYRIGHT
Wright Tyndale & van Roden Inc ENGLAND transfer printed in blue in both script and
capitals (backstamp 7). This was presumably an American retailer.
Although not advertised until 1932, with Delphinium Chintz being advertised in *The Pottery Gazette* in 1931, Summertime was the second chintz pattern to be issued by Grimwades. The trade press was almost lyrical in its praise and a report in *The Pottery Gazette* in July 1932 reads, 'The trade will recall the old 'Marguerite Chintz', which, not many years ago, was a tremendous success.

This has now been succeeded by a pattern which has been christened 'Summertime'. It is a sort of fantasia, compounded of roses, daisies, violets, harebells, and similar summer-time flowers. This is said to have been taken up freely by many of the leading buyers, some of whom have not hesitated to pronounce it even an improvement upon the old 'Marguerite'; and to say that is to say a good deal.'

The pattern features all the flowers mentioned above, but the violets are rather indistinguishable. It was also issued in a different colourway as Bedale, with the pattern featuring the roses in yellow and not pink.

Group A	Group B	Group C	Group D
£35-£60	£70-£85	£125-£225	£425-£625
$60-$115	$125-$165	$220-$440	$745-$1225

Sunshine c1930s (picture page 47)
Pattern number 4030
Backstamp 4
A warmly coloured pattern evocative of its name, Sunshine has large anemone-like flowers in blue and in pink, with the petals shading to yellow, accompanied by smaller dark blue and white flowers and forget-me-nots. The green leaves and flowers have yellow shading merging with the minimal white ground.

Group A	Group B	Group C	Group D
£25-£40	£60-£90	£125-£225	£400-£550
$45-$80	$105-$175	$220-$440	$700-$1075

Sweet Nancy c1930s-1940s (picture page 47)
Pattern number 5828
Backstamp 4
Bouquets of white narcissi and what appear to be wallflowers are the theme of this design. Background flowers resembling lilacs are accompanied by tiny yellow flowers set against a cream ground

Group A	Group B	Group C	Group D
£35-£55	£60-£80	£125-£195	£400-£600
$60-$110	$105-$155	$220-$380	$700-$1175

Sweet Pea 1936 (picture pages 47, 48, 49 and 50)
Pattern number 3030
Backstamp 4
Registration number Australia 15538
Vivid blossoms of the sweet pea in colours of pink, deep blue, deep yellow and white are arranged against a background of leaves and coiling tendrils. The ground colour varies from a pale cream to a deep yellow/ochre.

An invoice from Grimwades to Queen Mary, dated the 15th July 1936, shows that Her Majesty ordered tea pot number 12, Athena shape, in this pattern, priced at 2/- (10p) and a salad bowl and servers No 2 and No 2A in King shape at a cost of 3/6d (17½p).

Group A	Group B	Group C	Group D
£50-£85	£95-£155	£225-£350	£600-£875
$90-$165	$165-$305	$395-$685	$1050-$1715

'Sweet Pea II' c1930s (picture page 50)
Pattern number 4461
Backstamp 4
This is unlike the earlier Sweet Pea pattern (see previous) both in colour and design, The later flowers are slightly more clearly outlined, with the leaves more finely drawn. The sweet peas are portrayed in English cottage garden colours of pinkish-mauve with additional blooms in the unusual colour of yellow ochre. The pattern stands out well against the creamy white ground.

Group A	Group B	Group C	Group D
£50-£90	£125-£250	£350-£500	£700-£800
$90-$175	$220-$490	$615-$980	$1225-$1565

Tartans c1937 (picture page 50)
Pattern number 4514
Backstamp 6
Registration number GB 824091 (c1937); Canada 23.12.37 (which appears to be a date); Australia 17468
Various overlapping scraps of plaids in bright colours form the basis of this pattern. Combined colours of blue, green, scarlet, orange and beige are crossed and bisected with lines of yellow, black, blue, green and white, giving an attractive but jumbled effect.

Group A	Group B	Group C	Group D
£20-£40	£60-£95	£125-£200	£250-£375
$35-$80	$105-$185	$220-$390	$440-$735

'Tea Roses' c1917 (picture page 50)
Pattern number (possibly) 4252
Backstamp 1
A pretty example of an early chintz pattern. The colours are muted, yet vibrant, with roses done in shades of pink and lilac, with other flowers picked out in yellow, orange and pink. The rose leaves are green and added colour is given by tiny fern-like leaves in blue.

Group A	Group B	Group C	Group D
£20-£40	£60-£95	£125-£200	£400-£500
$35-$80	$105-$185	$220-$390	$700-$980

Triumph 1939 (picture page 51)
Pattern number 112
Backstamp 4. Also marked GRIMWADES MADE IN ENGLAND transfer printed in green.
Bunches of yellow and blue crocuses, together with sprays of pink and blue flowers, are set against a black ground. The pattern is identical to White Crocus apart from the ground colour.

Items in this pattern were exhibited at Olympia in 1939 and the Royal Winton stand was visited by Queen Mary, the Duke of Kent and the Princess Royal. The Royal party bought many pieces of ware including Triumph.

Group A	Group B	Group C	Group D
£35-£50	£90-£125	£155-£250	£350-£550
$60-$100	$160-$245	$270-$490	$615-$1075

Victorian c1930s (picture page 51)
Pattern number 3164
Backstamp 4
Another needlepoint or sampler pattern, Victorian is an alternative colourway to Queen Anne. The pattern consists of bouquets of flowers in pink, blue and yellow, accompanied by green leaves and executed in a cross-stitch effect. The graph paper effect is of white squares on a black ground.

Queen Mary ordered a Bowl No 3 in the Victorian pattern at a cost of 2/6d (12½p) and the invoice is dated the 15th July 1936.

Group A	Group B	Group C	Group D
£20-£40	£50-£90	£120-£175	£250-£325
$35-$80	$90-$175	$210-$345	$440-$635

Victorian Rose c1950s (picture page 52)
Pattern number 440
Backstamp 4, 8
Registration number Canada 1953
The pattern shows dark pink roses arranged in a bouquet with smaller flat blue flowers interspersed. An occasional half-opened yellow rosebud is also seen. The flowers are fairly widely spaced against the white ground.

Group A	Group B	Group C	Group D
£30-£70	£100-£200	£275-£400	£500-£625
$55-$135	$175-$390	$480-$7825	$875-$1225

'Violets' c1930s (picture page 52)
Backstamp 4
An extremely pretty design of purple violets and vivid yellow primroses, delicately enhanced by green and pale purple leaves. The ground colour is ivory.

Group A	Group B	Group C	Group D
£20-£45	£60-£115	£150-£250	£400-£500
$35-$90	$105-$225	$265-$490	$700-$980

Welbeck c1930s (picture pages 52, 54, 58 and 59)
Pattern number 2204
Backstamp 4
This shows a large bouquet of flowers consisting of pink and yellow roses, yellow daffodils and white narcissi. Pale lilac tulips and purple wisteria, rather indistinctly coloured, edge the bouquet which is interspersed with delicate green leaves.

The same pattern features in both Hazel and Spring but against differently coloured backgrounds. The ground colour of Welbeck is yellow, irregularly partitioned by small pebble shapes in ochre.

Group A	Group B	Group C	Group D
£65-£95	£90-£160	£145-£475	£1000-£1250
$115-$185	$160-$315	$255-$930	$1750-$2445

'White Roses' (picture page 54)
Pattern number possibly 1575
Backstamp 8
Roses, shaded in white and grey, are seen scattered across a lemon yellow ground. Small grey and even smaller black leaves highlight the ground colour.

Group A	Group B	Group C	Group D
£20-£35	£50-£90	£125-£175	£200-£295
$35-$70	$90-$175	$220-$345	$350-$580

Wild Flowers c1930s (picture page 54)
Pattern number 3149
Backstamp 4, 5
Wild flowers are scattered across what seems to be a background of yellow mimosa balls. The white flowers are unidentifiable but the blue spray is probably Wood Vetch, while the flat pink flower closely resembles the Dianthus armeria known as Deptford pink.

Group A	Group B	Group C	Group D
£45-£75	£80-£110	£100-£250	£250-£850
$80-$145	$140-$215	$175-$490	$440-$1665

Winifred c1950s (picture page 54)
Backstamp Royal Winton in script accompanied by Grimwades Made in England
This chintz pattern is portrayed in autumnal colours. Half-opened and open roses in subdued shades of yellow, rust and pink are dominated by olive green leaves and tiny brown leaves, all set against a white ground.

Group A	Group B	Group C	Group D
£20-£35	£50-£90	£125-£175	£200-£295
$35-$70	$90-$175	$220-$345	$350-$580

JAMES KENT LTD (OLD FOLEY)
Established 1897, Old Foley Pottery, Longton, Staffordshire

JK1 1913+

JK2 1930s+

JK3
1930s

JK4 1930s+

JK5
1936-1939

Apple Blossom (picture page 59)
Date of manufacture 1930s
Backstamp JK3
Clusters of apple blossom in various shades of pink and white decorate the white ground. Green leaves and small blue and yellow flowers give additional colour.

Group A	Group B	Group C	Group D
£40-£60	£65-£75	£70-£160	£375-£500
$70-$115	$115-$145	$125-$315	$655-$980

'Autumn Flowers' (picture page 60)
Date of manufacture 1930s
Backstamp JK5
A rather abstract pattern of stylised flowers in autumn colours of yellow, blue and rust. Accompanying leaves are in green, black, rust and yellow. The ground colour is white with sepia blocking at random.

Group A	Group B	Group C	Group D
£30-£45	£60-£90	£125-£200	£300-£400
$55-$90	$105-$175	$220-$390	$525-$785

Crazy Paving (picture page 60)
Date of manufacture 1930s – Pattern number 2939
Backstamp JK2
This is a delicate pattern of miniature pink roses, pink tulips, yellow and pink primulas, bright blue asters and other spring flowers. The ground colour is white with random patterns in beige representing the crazy paving.

Group A	Group B	Group C	Group D
£30-£45	£60-£90	£125-£200	£350-£500
$55-$90	$105-$175	$220-$390	$615-$980

Du Barry (picture pages 60 and 61)
Date of manufacture 1930s+
Backstamp JK2, JK3
Du Barry is perhaps the most recognisable of the Kent patterns. A profusion of briar roses in shades of pink, yellow and white, are accompanied by pale blue daisies. The overall effect is colourful but predominantly pink.

Group A	Group B	Group C	Group D
£45-£65	£60-£85	£100-£225	£475-£600
$80-$125	$105-$165	$175-$440	$830-$1175

Florita (picture page 61)
Date of manufacture Late 1950s – Pattern number 5008
Backstamp JK4, and as JK but with a crown above
One of the more popular Kent patterns, it consists of briar roses, daisies and other flat-petalled flowers accompanied by a few small green leaves and set on a black ground. The colours are bright and pretty, comprising blue, white and pink shading, yellow and a vivid cerise pink.

Group A	Group B	Group C	Group D
£40-£65	£70-£90	£95-£175	£475-£650
$70-$125	$125-$175	$165-$345	$830-$1275

Harmony (See T. G. Green picture on page 22)
An open stock pattern that was used by several companies, including T. G. Green, Hollinshead & Kirkham, and A. G. Richardson (Crown Ducal).
Tea Roses are shown in shades of pale orange, peach and yellow, with narcissi in white. Other unidentifiable flowers are in blue and pale orange. Pale green leaves accompany the bouquets of flowers and the ground colour is white.

Group A	Group B	Group C	Group D
£20-£35	£35-£45	£50-£95	£225-£350
$35-$70	$60-$90	$90-$185	$395-$685

Hydrangea (Black) (picture page 61)
Date of manufacture 1930s+
Backstamp JK2, JK3, JK1; 1955+ Old Foley in script above JAMES KENT LTD STAFFORDSHIRE MADE IN ENGLAND with the pattern name in script set within quotes
Although it bears the same pattern name as Hydrangea (White), there are subtle differences between the two patterns, quite apart from colouring. The black version shows the hydrangea flower rather poorly defined in shades of pink, blue and ochre. Broad leaves of the plant are depicted in green and ochre, while narrow leaves totally unrelated to the hydrangea are shown in green. The ground colour is black.

Group A	Group B	Group C	Group D
£25-£45	£50-£90	£100-£200	£275-£400
$45-$90	$90-$175	$175-$390	$305-$785

Hydrangea (White) (picture page 61)
Date of manufacture 1930s+
Backstamp as Hydrangea (Black)
Although this is sometimes claimed to be a different colourway of the Hydrangea pattern, the assumption is incorrect as there are subtle differences between the two (see above). The 'white' colourway shows finely drawn blooms in deep pink, white, outlined in blue, and lilac, accompanied by broad leaves in green and a pale blue-grey. The narrow leaves shown in Hydrangea (Black) are missing. The ground colour is a pale primrose.

Group A	Group B	Group C	Group D
£40-£65	£75-£100	£150-£300	£550-£650
$70-$125	$130-$195	$265-$585	$965-$1275

Lichfield (see W.R. Midwinter)

Marigold (picture page 62)
Date of manufacture 1930s
Backstamp JK4
Vivid colours of orange, blue and green make this pattern stand out. French marigolds in orange are accompanied by shaded yellow daisies, while bright blue cornflowers make for a colour contrast.

Group A	Group B	Group C	Group D
£25-£40	£45-£55	£60-£95	£275-£325
$45-$80	$80-$110	$105-$185	$480-$635

Mille Fleurs (picture page 62)
Date of manufacture 1930s
Backstamp JK2, JK3
This was an open stock pattern and can also be seen on wares made by A. G. Richardson (Crown Ducal). It was also issued by Elijah Cotton (Lord Nelson Ware) who called it Marigold.
   The pattern shows a variety of summer flowers in various shades of yellow, pink and blue, all with green leaves and set on a white ground. The flowers consist mainly of French marigolds, narcissi, campanula (bell flowers) and flat-petalled roses.

Group A	Group B	Group C	Group D
£35-£45	£45-£55	£70-£120	£325-£425
$60-$90	$80-$110	$125-$235	$570-$830

Primula (picture page 62)
Date of manufacture 1930s
Backstamp JK3
The pattern is almost entirely covered with flowers, with very little of the white ground showing. Yellow primroses are set against their green leaves, while purple violets peep from behind.

Group A	Group B	Group C	Group D
£40-£65	£75-£85	£90-£165	£395-£500
$70-$125	$130-$165	$160-$325	$690-$980

Rapture (picture page 63)
Date of manufacture 1930s
Backstamp JK3, JK4
This is a rather open and delicate pattern. Tea roses are seen in shades of pink along with purple irises and other unidentifiable flowers in purple and yellow. Apple-green leaves intersperse the blooms and the ground colour is white.

Group A	Group B	Group C	Group D
£40-£60	£55-£125	£150-£200	£300-£450
$70-$115	$95-$245	$265-$390	$525-$880

Rosalynde (picture page 63)
Date of manufacture 1930s+
Backstamp JK4
Large cabbage roses in pink, with smaller ones in yellow, form the main part of this design. Yellow anemones can also be seen along with bright blue Speedwells or Forget-Me-Nots. Other flowers are in yellow and pink. Leaves are mainly green, with additional sprays of tiny yellow leaves. The pattern is an open one, and has a light and airy feel to it.

Group A	Group B	Group C	Group D
£40-£65	£65-£75	£75-£165	£425-£650
$70-$125	$115-$145	$130-$325	$745-$1275

Roses (picture page 63)
Date of manufacture 1930s – Pattern number 3084
Backstamp JK4
An open sheet pattern of pink tea roses together with small buds and green leaves is set against a white ground. The rim is gilded in a 'cloud' effect.

Group A	Group B	Group C	Group D
£30-£40	£60-£90	£120-£200	£300-£400
$55-$80	$105-$175	$210-$390	$525-$785

Silverdale (picture page 64)
Date of manufacture 1930s – Pattern number 1097
Backstamp JK3 (pattern name in capital letters, not italics)
Bluebells, orange tulips, and other flowers in blue and orange are interspersed by tiny scrolling leaves in dark green and tan. Cerise dots are found in clusters here and there. There was also an open stock pattern and was used by other companies, such as Royal Winton.

Group A	Group B	Group C	Group D
£30-£40	£50-£60	£60-£90	£250-£350
$55-$80	$90-$115	$105-$175	$440-$685

Tapestry (picture page 64)
Date of manufacture 1950s
Pattern number 5615
Backstamp Old Foley in script above JAMES KENT LTD STAFFORDSHIRE MADE IN ENGLAND. The pattern name is in script below
A striking arrangement of bright cerise roses and lilac together with green rose leaves, set against a black ground.

Group A	Group B	Group C	Group D
£35-£50	£50-£65	£70-£140	£325-£500
$60-$100	$90-$125	$125-$275	$570-$980

18th Century Chintz (picture page 64)
Date of manufacture 1913+
Backstamp JK1
This is a copy of an 18th century chintz design and is a rather open pattern. Deep pink roses are combined with blue flax flower heads and with what appears to be a purple dahlia. This spray is widely arranged against a background of delicately traced lilac-shaded flower outlines set on a white ground. In addition, there are sprays of roses, dark blue convolvulus, tiny yellow flowers, with other flowers in purple.

Group A	Group B	Group C	Group D
£30-£40	£60-£90	£120-£200	£300-£400
$55-$80	$105-$175	$210-$390	$525-$785

LEIGHTON POTTERY LTD (ROYAL LEIGHTON WARE)
In existence 1940-54, Orme Street, Burslem, Staffordshire

'Autumn Roses' (picture page 64)
Date of manufacture 1940s
Backstamp as illustration
A few manufacturers combined chintz with broad bands of solid colour, perhaps to offset the rather overwhelming effect of the busy pattern. Leighton Pottery combined the massed bronze roses with a ground colour of pale turquoise.

Group A	Group B	Group C	Group D
£30-£40	£60-£90	£120-£200	£300-£400
$55-$80	$105-$175	$210-$390	$525-$785

W. R. MIDWINTER LTD
Established 1910, Albion and Hadderidge Potteries, Burslem, Staffordshire

MIDWINTER
ENGLAND
STAFFORDSHIRE
SEMI-PORCELAIN
**A CORAL PLATE
PRODUCT**

RE ENGLAND
FASHION SHAPE
3-62

Mid 1   *Mid 2: 1940s+*   *Mid 3: 1950s+*

Brama (picture page 64)
Date of manufacture 1940s+
Backstamp 1 – MIDWINTER BURSLEM set within the boundaries of two circles with PORCELAIN bisecting the circles horizontally. ENGLAND below and the letter B above (not illustrated). Backstamp 2 – Mid 2 with pattern name of BRAMA, set in quotes, is also sometimes found
This pattern was originally issued under the title of Springtime, the name being later changed to Brama in the late 1940s. The reason for the change is, unfortunately, unknown.

It is perhaps one of the most well-known of the Midwinter patterns. Large peony-type blooms in shaded pink are seen against a background of daffodils, tulips, harebells and other spring flowers in yellow, pink and blue. Green leaves accompany the flowers and the ground colour is white.

Group A	Group B	Group C	Group D
£50-£55	£60-£80	£90-£145	£250-£300
$90-$110	$105-$155	$160-$285	$440-$585

Coral (picture page 64)
Date of manufacture 1940s+
Backstamp Mid 2, Mid 3 with date stamp i.e. 3-62
Pink and white apple blossom, together with yellow and white daisies and blue forget-me-nots, are arranged in branches and sprays for this pattern, giving it a spring-like look. The ground colour is white, enhanced by the green leaves of the apple tree.

Group A	Group B	Group C	Group D
£45-£55	£60-£75	£85-£165	£225-£300
$80-$110	$105-$145	$150-$325	$395-$585

Lichfield (picture page 65)
Date of manufacture 1940s+
Backstamp none
This pattern can be found on known Midwinter shapes and on items by James Kent. Sprays of narrow leaves form the greater part of the manner and these are in shades of green and ochre, with touches of scarlet. Broader leaves are in scarlet, mauve-grey, ochre and black. Softening these rather stark colours are sprays of heather in muted tones of pink. The ground colour is white.

Group A	Group B	Group C	Group D
£30-£35	£35-£45	£50-£100	£250-£350
$55-$70	$60-$90	$90-$195	$440-$685

Lorna Doone (picture page 17)
Date of manufacture 1960s+
Backstamp 1, Mid 1, Mid 3
This pattern is difficult to date and was also used by other factories, such as Barker Brothers Ltd. A full page advertisement was inserted in *Pottery Gazette* by A. J. Wilkinson in May 1949 which praised the new Lorna Doone design. It was also produced by Midwinter under their Stylecraft backstamp which dates from 1961, although Midwinter probably did not use the pattern until after they took over Wilkinson's in 1964. The Midwinter pattern appears to also later have been called 'Bird Chintz' with some American collectors calling it 'Chickadee'.

Lorna Doone is an open pattern and depicts small birds in blue and yellow perched on branches of what appear to be rose bushes. The flowers are picked out in shades of pink, yellow and blue. Tiny blue and grey dots arranged randomly or in leaf shapes help obscure the white ground.

Group A	Group B	Group C	Group D
£35-£45	£45-£60	£60-£125	£200-£300
$60-$90	$80-$115	$105-$245	$350-$585

Springtime – *See Brama*

MYOTT SON & COMPANY LTD
Established 1898, Alexander Pottery, Stoke (Cobridge 1902-46) (Hanley 1947+)

MYOTT

STAFFORDSHIRE
ENGLAND

Bermuda (picture page 65)
Date of manufacture 1930s
Backstamp as illustrated
A bold and rather striking design can be seen on this pattern. Large yellow tea roses are set against brown leaves with occasional dashes of red/orange enamelling.

Group A	Group B	Group C	Group D
£20-£30	£25-£40	£35-£95	£125-£160
$35-$60	$45-$80	$60-$185	$220-$315

'Spring Flower' (picture page 65)
Date of manufacture 1930s – Pattern number 3005
Backstamp as illustration
This pattern was also used by Paragon China and Wilkinsons, either as an all-over pattern or in bands on teaware. No ground colour can be seen beneath the riot of vividly coloured flowers. The main flowers are tulips in pink or yellow shading to flame, dark blue scilla, and pale yellow narcissi accented with orange centres. Other unidentifiable flowers are in pale and dark blue and pink. The foliage is a bright grassy green.

Group A	Group B	Group C	Group D
£45-£50	£60-£70	£125-£200	£350-£400
$80-$100	$105-$135	$220-$390	$615-$785

Summer Flower (picture page 65)
Date of manufacture 1930s
Backstamp as illustration
This is a rather more open pattern than 'Spring Flowers', with the white ground showing clearly. Two-tone irises in pink and blue are accompanied by columbines in a deeper pink and yellow. Blue forget-me-nots, pink poppies and other small-petalled flowers are seen in yellow, pink and blue, the whole offset by green leaves.

Group A	Group B	Group C	Group D
£45-£60	£80-£100	£125-£220	£350-£400
$80-$115	$140-$195	$220-$430	$615-$785

PARAGON: China Co. LTD (formerly Star China Co)
Established 1920, Atlas Works, Longton, Staffordshire

June Glory (picture page 66)
Date of manufacture 1930s
Backstamp as illustration
A rather vaguely drawn pattern, with flat-petalled flowers in shades of pale primrose with deeper yellow centres. The flowers and green leaves are set on a soft lilac-pink ground.

Group A	Group B	Group C	Group D
£30-£40	£60-£90	£120-£200	£300-£400
$55-$80	$105-$175	$210-$390	$525-$785

'Spring Flower'
See Myott picture page 65
This pattern was also used by Myott and Wilkinsons, and can be found on Paragon China, either as an all-over pattern or in bands on teaware.

No ground colour can be seen beneath the riot of vividly coloured flowers. The main flowers are tulips in pink or yellow shading to flame, dark blue scilla, and pale yellow narcissi accented with orange centres. Other unidentifiable flowers are in pale and dark blue and pink. The foliage is a bright grassy green.

Group A	Group B	Group C	Group D
£30-£40	£60-£90	£120-£200	£300-£400
$55-$80	$105-$175	$210-$390	$525-$785

A. G. RICHARDSON Co LTD (CROWN DUCAL)
Established 1915, Gordon Pottery, Tunstall, Staffordshire

AG1: 1916+
This mark can be
found with or
without A.G.R.
and Co Ltd
ENGLAND below.

AG2: 1916+,
as AG1 but
coloured in red
and yellow.
MADE IN ENGLAND
above and below.

AG3: 1925+

AG4: 1930+
Sometimes Made in
England replaces
England

Ascot (picture page 66)
Date of manufacture 1916 – Pattern number 404
Backstamp AG1; AG3; AG4
A rather open pattern set on a white ground which is decorated with random dots of blue. Roses are done in shades of pink, together with yellow flowers and dark blue stylised blossoms. The leaves are a dark green and the branches are brown.

Group A	Group B	Group C	Group D
£45-£50	£70-£90	£120-£200	£275-£400
$80-$100	$125-$175	$210-$390	$480-$785

Blue Chintz (picture page 66)
Date of manufacture 1925+
Backstamp AG3
Branching sprays of many-petalled flowers in shades of pink and white are set off by the dramatic blue ground. A brilliantly plumed bird, picked out in yellow and green, with his sweeping tail in rust and yellow, can be found perched on a branch. Small lilac daisies and sprays of apple blossom, together with green leaves also form part of the pattern.

Group A	Group B	Group C	Group D
£50-£60	£65-£90	£120-£200	£400-£500
$90-$115	$115-$175	$210-$390	$700-$980

Canton (picture page 66)
Date of manufacture 1925+ – Pattern number 404
Backstamp AG3
A lively pattern showing Chinese lanterns in shades of yellow and rust swinging from branches of pine trees. The pattern receives its impact from the rich blue ground.

Group A	Group B	Group C	Group D
£35-£45	£45-£65	£60-£185	£225-£325
$60-$90	$80-$125	$105-$360	$395-$635

Festival (picture page 66)
Date of manufacture 1925+
Backstamp AG3
This shows influences of the Canton pattern with its Chinese lanterns. However, the pattern is much lighter in design. Small lanterns hang here and there from branches bearing flowers in an assortment of shapes and colours. Deep blue, cerise and orange are combined, with pale blue,lilac and yellow. The leaves in dark blue and green and the whole is set against a white ground, broken slight by small pale grey leaves.

Group A	Group B	Group C	Group D
£40-£50	£50-£75	£125-£225	£325-£400
$70-$100	$90-$145	$220-$440	$570-$785

Florida (picture page 67)
Date of manufacture 1925+
Backstamp AG3 1925+
Subdued shades of a pinky-grey mauve, separated by fine darker lines of colour, form the background to this pattern which is also known to American collectors as Mauve Crown Ducal not to be confused with Mauve Chintz. Two birds with brightly coloured yellow and blue breasts and yellow tail feathers are perched on a branch, bare except for three orange berries. Clusters of dark red blackcurrants and bunches of small blue berries are set below pale yellow roses. The pattern has an autumnal feel to it.

Group A	Group B	Group C	Group D
£40-£50	£75-£150	£200-£300	£500-£650
$70-$100	$130-$295	$350-$585	$875-$1275

'Grey Fruit' (picture page 67)
Date of manufacture 1916+ – Pattern number (possibly) 1011404
Backstamp AG1, AG3
A dull grey background shows up the autumn fruit on this pattern. The branches are dark blue or navy, the leaves are green and small pink and white flowerheads are scattered here and there. The fruits, which appear to be plums, are in shades of yellow and a deep pink.

Group A	Group B	Group C	Group D
£30-£40	£45-£60	£75-£120	£200-£350
$55-$80	$80-$115	$130-$235	$350-$685

Ivory Chintz (picture page 67)
Date of manufacture 1916+ – Pattern number 500
Backstamp AG1
When closely examined, this is an extremely pretty and interesting pattern. Large flowerheads in varying shades of pale and deep pink, enhanced with mauve, are set against green foliage of diverse shapes. An occasional rust anemone with a blue centre can also be found, together with stylised blue flowers. Pale purple blackberries tip the branches and, in complete contrast, a parrot-like bird can be found with wings half-extended. The whole is set on a white ground.

   Some of the patterns vary slightly, additional tiny flowerheads in blues and pinks occupy some of the white space, making the pattern look denser and more brightly coloured. It is not known why this occurs.

Group A	Group B	Group C	Group D
£50-£65	£75-£110	£125-£200	£300-£450
$90-$125	$130-$215	$220-$390	$525-$880

'Ivory Fruit' (picture page 67)

Date of manufacture 1925+
Backstamp AG3

Scarlet and orange cherry-like fruit are seen clustered against blue-green and grey leaves. Small flower heads in yellow and orange give the pattern added interest, and the whole is set against a white ground.

Group A	Group B	Group C	Group D
£40-£55	£60-£75	£90-£150	£175-£325
$70-$110	$105-$145	$160-$295	$305-$635

Marigold (picture page 67)

Date of manufacture 1925+ – Pattern number 1063
Backstamp AG3

Mainly used for ornamental ware such as vases and bowls, Marigold is a striking pattern. the French marigold is portrayed in a bright naturalistic orange enhanced by a few green leaves. the background is done in shades of light and dark purple.

Group A	Group B	Group C	Group D
£40-£50	£55-£70	£100-£200	£275-£400
$70-$100	$95-$135	$175-$390	$305-$785

'Mauve Chintz'

Date of manufacture 1925+
Backstamp AG4

An open stock pattern, this is nevertheless associated mostly with Crown Ducal. The background colour is of a sharp mauve and is intensely striking. The flowers are tea roses in yellow, shaded with red, while an exotic bird, its plumage in dark blue and scarlet, clings to slender branch.

Group A	Group B	Group C	Group D
£45-£50	£60-£80	£90-£140	£250-£350
$80-$100	$105-$155	$160-$275	$440-$685

'Mille Fleurs' (picture page 68)

Date of manufacture 1930s
Backstamp AG4

This is an open stock pattern and can also be seen on ware made by James Kent when it was called Mille Fleurs. It was also issued by Elijah Cotton (Lord Nelson Ware) who called it Marigold.

The pattern shows a variety of summer flowers in various shades of yellow, pink and blue, all with green leaves and set on a white ground. the flowers consist mainly of French marigolds, narcissi, campanula (bell flowers) and flat-petalled roses.

Group A	Group B	Group C	Group D
£40-£70	£90-£150	£175-£350	£500-£600
$70-$135	$160-$295	$305-$685	$875-$1175

Peony (picture page 68)
Date of manufacture 1937 – Pattern number 5008
Backstamp AG3, AG4
Peony-like flowers in pale pink, shading to a darker hue, together with other blossoms in pink, white and yellow, form this pattern. Apple-green leaves form the background, along with smaller, stylised flowerheads in white outlined in a grey-blue. The ground colour is white.

Group A	Group B	Group C	Group D
£55-£65	£60-£80	£95-£175	£300-£450
$95-$125	$105-$155	$165-$345	$525-$880

'Pink Chintz' (picture page 68)
Date of manufacture 1925+ – Pattern number 404
Backstamp AG2, AG3, AG4
The vivid pinks used as colouring for the flowers make this an extremely attractive pattern. Pink roses and pale chrysanthemums, accompanied by yellow dahlia-like flowers are set against a forest of rose and chrysanthemum leaves, behind which the yellow ground appears at intervals.

Group A	Group B	Group C	Group D
£40-£65	£75-£110	£125-£200	£275-£400
$70-$125	$130-$195	$245-$390	$480-$785

Primula (picture page 68)
Date of manufacture 1930s – Pattern number (possibly) 4488
Backstamp AG3
Sprays of vivid yellow primulas, together with their characteristic leaves, decorate the creamy white ground on this pattern. The pattern has an appealing freshness about it

Group A	Group B	Group C	Group D
£50-£75	£75-£90	£100-£175	£225-£375
$90-$145	$130-$175	$175-$345	$395-$735

Priscilla
Date of manufacture 1940
Backstamp AG3 plus Made In England in script
Quite a delicate and almost subdued pattern, Priscilla was hailed by *The Pottery Gazette* in 1941 as "an all-over Chintz in pink apple blossom applied to a delicate buff ground, and broken up with small white speedwell flower heads". The groups of flower heads are spaced quite widely apart, giving the pattern an airy feel

Group A	Group B	Group C	Group D
£35-£50	£55-£70	£95-£130	£175-£325
$60-$100	$95-$135	$165-$255	$305-$635

"Purple Chintz"
Date of manufacture c1930s
Backstamp AG3
The design includes dramatic colours, set on a clear white ground. Many-petalled flowers are set on branches and done in colours of pink, red, indigo, yellow and purple. The accompanying leaves are green. Easily missed in this busy pattern is a small cock bird in shades of mauve and purple.

Group A	Group B	Group C	Group D
£75-£90	£85-£100	£125-£250	£450-£600
$130-$175	$150-$195	$220-$490	$790-$1175

RIDGWAYS (BEDFORD WORKS) LTD
In existence 1920–1952, Bedford Works, Shelton, Hanley Staffordshire

Rid 1   *Rid 2*
Sometimes the date mark is impressedSometimes England is replaced by Made in England (i.e. 1.9.38)

'Autumn Flowers' (picture page 68)
Date of manufacture 1930s
Backstamp Rid 1
A busy but attractive pattern in autumn colours of pink, ochre, rust and white, with varying shades of green being used for the leaves; no ground colour is shown. The flowers are mainly large cabbage roses, chrysanthemums and various stylised blooms.

Group A	Group B	Group C	Group D
£30-£50	£75-£120	£175-£250	£400-£500
$55-$100	$130-$235	$305-$490	$700-$980

'Poppies' (picture page 69)
Date of manufacture 1950s
Backstamp Rid 2
A pale primrose yellow ground offsets the green leaves and pink and white colours of the flowers in this pattern. Close examination reveals that the flowers are, in fact, poppies which makes the choice of colouring unusual (and incorrect).

Group A	Group B	Group C	Group D
£30-£50	£75-£120	£175-£250	£400-£500
$55-$100	$130-$235	$305-$490	$700-$980

RIDGWAYS POTTERIES LTD
Established 1955, Ash Hall, Stoke, Staffordshire

Rid 3

'Summer Flowers' (picture page 69)
Date of manufacture 1960s
Backstamp Rid 3
A pretty pattern comprising roses in various shades of pink, together with blue harebells and flat-petalled flowers in pale rust, blue and lilac. Leaves are green and sepia and are set against a white ground.

Group A	Group B	Group C	Group D
£30-£50	£75-£120	£175-£250	£400-£500
$55-$100	$130-$235	$305-$490	$700-$980

JOHN SHAW & SONS LONGTON LTD (BURLINGTON WARE)
In existence 1931–63, Willow Pottery, Longton, Staffordshire

'Anemone' See John Tams (picture page 71)
Date of manufacture 1930s
Anemone was an open stock pattern and was also used by Elijah Cotton (Lord Nelson Ware) and John Tams Ltd (Tams Ware) (Burlington Ware).
   Vividly coloured anemones, accompanied by green leaves are set on a white ground. The flowers are in blue, pink and yellow.

Group A	Group B	Group C	Group D
£35-£65	£70-£130	£180-£250	£400-£500
$60-$125	$125-$255	$315-$490	$700-$980

'Spring Daisies' (picture page 69)
Date of manufacture 1950s
Dramatic colourings are set against a black ground for this pattern. Daisies, harebells and other spring flowers are picked out in vivid blue, cerise, yellow and white tinged with pink.

Group A	Group B	Group C	Group D
£30-£50	£75-£120	£175-£250	£400-£500
$55-$100	$130-$235	$305-$490	$700-$980

SHELLEY (POTTERIES LTD)
Established 1925, The Foley, Longton, Staffordshire

Countryside
Date of manufacture 1940s
Backstamp Shelley in script set within a rectangular shield, with the pattern name below a riotous tangle of meadow flowers and berries make this pattern a positive delight. Pink clover can be identified, as can blue harebells, cornflowers, and Viola Lutea (Mountain Pansy) in maroon and pale blue. The fruit would appear to be raspberries.

Group A	Group B	Group C	Group D
£65-£85	£85-£135	£140-£160	£500-£600
$115-$165	$150-$265	$245-$315	$875-$1175

Green Daisy (picture page 69)
Date of manufacture 1940s
Back stamp Shelley in capital letters set within a simplified shield
A sheet-patterned Chintz, Green Daisy is laid out in a way that gives it almost a wallpaper effect. This is aided by the long dark green stalks that connect each flower. The daisies, white with a cheerful yellow centre, are set against a ground of tiny green leaves.

Group A	Group B	Group C	Group D
£50-£60	£65-£85	£100-£175	£450-£500
$90-$115	$115-$70	$175-$345	$790-$980

Maytime (picture page 69)
Date of manufacture 1940s
Pattern number 12830
Registered number 771299
Backstamp 1925-45 Shelley in script within an elongated shield with ENGLAND below.
Sprays of apple blossom are shown in white and pink, accompanied by deeper pink buds. These are set off by green leaves and pale brown branches. The ground colour is white.

Group A	Group B	Group C	Group D
£45-£60	£75-£95	£110-£135	£550-£600
$80-$115	$130-$185	$195-$265	$965-$1175

Melody (picture page 70)
Date of manufacture 1940s
Backstamp as Green Daisy
A pale green ground decorated with white 'vermicelli' patterns set off this delicate pattern. Bouquets of daisies, cornflowers and other blossoms are picked out in pale primrose, pink, blue and rust. Occasional narrow-leafed stems add interest.

Group A	Group B	Group C	Group D
£35-£50	£70-£115	£125-£175	£650-£700
$60-$100	$125-$225	$220-$345	$1140-$1370

Pink Summer Glory (Morning Glory) (picture page 70)
Date of manufacture 1940s
Backstamp as Summer Glory
Although the pattern was once advertised as, and for many years called Pink Clover, this pattern is increasing becoming known as Pink Summer Glory as it carries the Summer Glory backstamp. The sprays of blossom are in keeping with Hydrangeas or Lilacs and the sprays of the flowers are set in bouquets across the pale pink ground. The colours used for the blooms are white, pink, blue and lilac, shading to mauve. The leaves are a blue-green and there are also narrow-leaved sprays in grey.

Group A	Group B	Group C	Group D
£65-£70	£75-£115	£120-£175	£500-£600
$95-$135	$130-$225	$210-$345	$875-$1175

Primrose
Date of manufacture 1940s
Backstamp as Rock Garden
Small bunches of primroses and their leaves contrast with the delicate pale blue ground. This is broken up by tiny speedwell flower heads. Gold trim valued slightly more.

Group A	Group B	Group C	Group D
£55-£65	£85-£125	£150-£225	£600-£700
$95-$125	$150-$245	$265-$440	$1050-$1370

Rock Garden (picture page 70)
Date of manufacture 1940s
Backstamp as Maytime
Crazy paving and boulders in muted shades of a pinky-beige form the background to this attractive pattern. The flowers are arranged in 'cushions' and comprise miniature and dwarf plants such as pink roses and sedum, yellow narcissi, blue campanula, and so on. A variety of foliage complements the pastel colours. Gold trim valued slightly more.

Group A	Group B	Group C	Group D
£55-£65	£85-£125	£150-£225	£600-£700
$95-$125	$150-$245	$265-$440	$1050-$1370

Summer Glory
Date of manufacture 1940s
Backstamp as Countryside but with pattern name in a riband across a bouquet of flowers.
Sprays of either Hydrangeas or Lilac are set in bouquets across a beige ground that is heightened by a white vermicelli design. Leaves are in brown and green, while the flower heads are in white, deep pink and shades of blue. The pattern can also be found in a pale pink colourway (see Pink Summer Glory when it is known to American collectors as Pink Clover.

Group A	Group B	Group C	Group D
£45-£65	£90-£125	£175-£250	£600-£700
$80-$125	$160-$245	$305-$490	$1050-$1370

SOHO POTTERY LTD (SOLIAN WARE)
Soho Pottery, Turnstall, Staffordshire
Established 1901

Sunningdale (picture page 70)
Date of manufacture 1930s
Backstamp 1930+ Solian Ware in script diagonally above SOHO POTTERY LTD. with COBRIDGE ENGLAND below
A very stylised pattern of leaves, fruits and flowers in autumnal shades. These comprise yellow, ochre, rust, maroon, lilac, pale blue, dark blue and a dull green. The ground colour is white.

Group A	Group B	Group C	Group D
£20-£30	£50-£80	£120-£200	£300-£400
$35-$60	$90-$155	$210-$390	$525-$785

'Tulips and Roses' (picture page 70)
Date of manufacture 1930s
Backstamp as 'Sunningdale'
Blue tulips and deep pink cabbage roses feature strongly in this pattern, along with blue tulips, pink carnations, yellow daisies, and what appears to be white mock orange blossom. Other flowers are depicted in shades of pink, mauve and lilac. The ground is white with small dots of grey.

Group A	Group B	Group C	Group D
£20-£30	£50-£80	£120-£200	£300-£400
$35-$60	$90-$155	$210-$390	$525-$785

JOHN TAMS LIMITED (TAMS WARE)

From 1912, Crown Pottery, Longton, Staffordshire

Tam 1: 1903+   *Tam 2: 1930+*

'Anemone' (picture page 71)
Date of manufacture 1930s
Backstamp Tam 1
Anemone was an open stock pattern and was freely used by other manufacturers including Elijah Cotton (Lord Nelson Ware), and J. Shaw (Burlington Ware). Vividly coloured anemones, accompanied by green leaves are set on a white ground. The flowers are in blue, pink and yellow.

Group A	Group B	Group C	Group D
£20-£30	£50-£80	£120-£200	£300-£400
$35-$60	$90-$155	$210-$390	$525-$785

'Blue Roses' (picture page 71)
Date of manufacture 1930s
Backstamp Tam 2
Full-blown roses and rosebuds are seen in pink, shaded with touches of yellow. The roses are infrequent, however, with a profusion of blue leaves creating the pattern. Touches of green and lime give additional colour.

Group A	Group B	Group C	Group D
£20-£40	£50-£80	£100-£200	£275-£395
$35-$80	$90-$155	$175-$390	$480-$775

WADE, HEATH + CO LTD
High Street Works (1927-38), Burslem, Staffordshire,
Royal Victoria Pottery (1938+), Burslem, Staffordshire

Wade 1 1939+   *Wade 2 1937+*

'Butterfly Chintz' (picture page 71)
Date of manufacture 1930s-1940s
Backstamp Wade 1
An extremely pretty pattern which has butterflies in colours of blue or rust and brown settling on a profusion of daisies and other flowers in shades of pink (pale and dark), yellow, white and blue.

Group A	Group B	Group C	Group D
£30-£45	£50-£60	£80-£100	£300-£400
$55-$90	$90-$115	$140-$195	$525-$785

Darwin (picture page 71)
Date of manufacture 1950s
Backstamp Wade 2
This self-coloured pattern is based on an early Davenport design of around 1835-1850. Davenport produced several chintz patterns in this period, such as Royal Chintz (sic). The Darwin pattern consists of sprays of leaves accompanied by blossoms and berries. The ground is made up of fine dots of colour against white.

Group A	Group B	Group C	Group D
£30-£45	£50-£60	£80-£100	£300-£400
$55-$90	$90-$115	$140-$195	$525-$785

Thistle Chintz (picture page 71)
Date of manufacture 1940s
Backstamp Wade 1
Sprays of the Meadow Thistle in shades of purple mingle with smaller sprays of yellow crocus. The muted colours are set on a cream ground with the green leaves of the thistle giving additional colour and interest.

Group A	Group B	Group C	Group D
£10-£40	£55-£80	£90-£140	£300-£450
$18-$80	$95-$155	$160-$275	$525-$880

J. H. WEATHERBY & SONS LTD (FALCON WARE)
Established 1891, Falcon Pottery, Hanley Staffs

'Peruvian Lily' (picture page 72)
Date of manufacture 1925+
Pattern number 7341
Backstamp Union Jack Durability flag with Weatherby Hanley England below and Falcon Ware in a curve
A colourful pattern, consisting of Peruvian Lilies in yellow and orange together with leaves in shades of green and ochre. Small pink and cerise blossoms and tiny blue flower heads give a softer effect. The ground colour is white.

Group A	Group B	Group C	Group D
£30-£55	£70-£125	£175-£250	£300-£400
$55-$110	$125-$245	$305-$490	$525-$785

WEDGWOOD & CO LTD (Union Pottery)
Established 1860, Unicorn and Pinnox Works, Tunstall, Staffordshire

'Columbine' (picture page 72)
Date of manufacture 1936+
Backstamp as illustration
Hardly any of the cream white ground shows through the profusion of columbines. The leaves are green and white, shading to pink, while the flowers are in blue and yellow, and cerise and yellow.

Group A	Group B	Group C	Group D
£30-£55	£70-£125	£175-£250	£300-£400
$55-$110	$125-$245	$305-$490	$525-$785

Cowslip (picture page 72)
Date of manufacture 1936+
Backstamp as illustration
Sprays of cowslips in a deep yellow, accompanied by green leaves, intermingle with small bunches of vivid blue flowers all of which is set on a creamy white ground. The overall effect is bright and fresh.

Group A	Group B	Group C	Group D
£30-£55	£60-£100	£150-£225	£300-£400
$55-$110	$105-$195	$265-$440	$525-$785

A. J. WILKINSON LTD (ROYAL STAFFORDSHIRE POTTERY)
Established 1885, Royal Staffordshire Pottery, Burslem, Staffordshire

Mayflower (picture page 72)
Date of manufacture c1950s
This would appear to be yet another open stock pattern, as it was also used by Myott Son & Co Ltd and Paragon China.
No ground colour can be seen beneath the riot of vividly coloured flowers. The main flowers are tulips in pink or yellow shading to flame, dark blue scilla, and pale yellow narcissi accented with orange centres. Other unidentifiable flowers are in pale and dark blue and pink. The foliage is a bright grassy green.

Group A	Group B	Group C	Group D
£30-£45	£50-£60	£70-£80	£90-£100
$55-$90	$90-$115	$125-$155	$160-$195

ARTHUR WOOD & SON (LONGPORT) LTD
Established 1928, Bradwell Works, Longport Staffordshire

Impressed ENGLAND and year marks also sometime appear

AW1 1934+

'Honeycomb Flowers' (picture page 72)
Date of manufacture 1936
Backstamp as illustration
A fine honeycomb design in pale brown set on a white ground forms the background. Green and brown branches carry various flowers such as poppies, peonies, convolvulus and daisies, all picked out in shades of deep pink and yellow. Small berries in purple and red give additional colour.

Group A	Group B	Group C	Group D
£30-£45	£50-£60	£70-£80	£90-£100
$55-$90	$90-$115	$125-$155	$160-$195

Francis Joseph

introduce

The Chintz Girls

An exclusive, limited series of figurines from Royal Winton incorporating famous patterns.
Handpainted by artists and only available direct from Francis Joseph London.
Please call us to place an order or to receive more details about other figures in the series

FREE

Collecting
Royal Winton
Chintz
with every order

Florence

Each figure is limited to 1000 only. £165/US$250 – available for international dispatch
at no extra charge. US custom welcome.
Tel International: (+44) 208 318 9580
UK: 0208 318 9580
Fax: 0208 318 1987
email: info@francisjoseph.co.uk

Francis Joseph
5 Southbrook Mews
London SE12 8LG

Francis Joseph
Collectors Register

Join the **Francis Joseph Chintz Collectors Register**. Registration is free and you will receive a newsletter twice yearly with news of auctions, events, sales and new publications on your particular collecting interest.

Join our Register by listing your top five Chintz designs and send it to:

The Francis Joseph Chintz Collectors Register
5 Southbrook Mews
London SE12 8LG

Art Deco

Christie's South Kensington is the only auction house to hold regular sales entirely devoted to Clarice Cliff, Carlton Ware, Poole Pottery, Susie Cooper, Charlotte Rhead and 20th Century Bronzes and Sculpture. For advice on all aspects of buying and selling Art Deco at auction or for a free verbal valuation and sales calendar please contact: Mark Wilkinson or Michael Jeffrey

0207-321 3236/3237

CHRISTIE'S

85 Old Brompton Road, London SW7 3LD
Tel: (0207) 581 7611   Fax: (0207) 321 3321

Francis Joseph

P U B L I C A T I O N S

'The Collectors' Choice'

Detailed price and information books on 20th century ceramics and glass with galleries of extensive colour photographs in each. All the collector needs for identifying the wide range of valuable ceramics and glass produced over the past 100 years.

Wade Collectors Handbook

First edition on this much sought after pottery. Hugely popular, this book lists all the most collectable pieces. Everything from whimsies to figures. **£12.95**

Collecting Pendelfin Second edition

This second edition is bigger, brighter, better. Full of pictures and a mine of information on one of the UKs best known and best loved collectables. Full of new information and up to date prices.

Collecting Shelley Pottery

Comprehensive and wide-reading first edition on one of the UKs leading and most tasteful potteries. Hundreds of colour pictures plus prices. **£16.95**

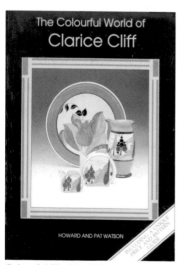

Colourful World of Clarice Cliff

Full colour book with up-to-date prices and hundreds of photographs. This book is ideal for all collectors and dealers alike. **£16.95**

Character Jug Collectors Handbook

Sixth Edition. Complete colour and price guide listing of all discontinued models. All Royal Doulton are listed along with other potteries. **£14.95**

The Bunnykins & Beatrix Potter Handbook

Price, picture and rarity guide of this now major collecting area. Royal Doulton, Beswick and Royal Albert all featured. Colour photographs throughout. **£14.95**

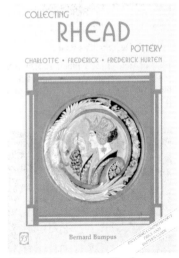

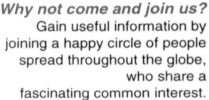